SUMMER LEARNING CRASH COURSE FOR MINECRAFTERS

GRADES 2-3

+ + +

Improve Core Subject Skills with Fun Activities

NANCY ROGERS BOSSE
ILLUSTRATED BY AMANDA BRACK

Sky Pony Press
New York

A NOTE TO PARENTS

You probably know the importance of having your child practice the key skills taught in the classroom. And you are probably hoping that your kid will be on board with practicing at home. Well, congratulations! You've come to the right place! *Summer Learning Crash Course for Minecrafters: Grades 2–3* transforms learning into an adventure complete with zombies, skeletons, and creepers.

You will love that *Summer Learning Crash Course for Minecrafters: Grades 2–3* aligns with the National Core Standards for math and English language arts (ELA), as well as national, state, and district recommendations for science and social studies. Every page reinforces a key concept in one of the subject areas. Your child will love the colorful art, familiar video game characters, and the fun approach to each learning activity!

The pages of this workbook are color coded to help you target specific skills areas as needed.

BLUE	**Language Arts**
ORANGE	**Math**
GREEN	**Science**
PINK	**Social Studies**

Whether it's the joy of seeing their favorite Minecraft characters on every page, the fun of solving a riddle or a puzzle, or the pride of accomplishment of completing a learning challenge, there is something in this book for even the most reluctant learner.

Happy adventuring!

  # CONTENTS

LONG OR SHORT VOWEL SOUND

Say each word. Listen for the vowel sound. Circle whether it is long or short.

1. beet

long   short

2. boat

long   short

3. run

long   short

4. ghast

long   short

5. head

long   short

6. blue

long   short

7. Steve

long   short

8. dog

long   short

9. axe

long   short

READING WORDS

Read each word. Draw a line to match the word to the picture.

1. beacon

A.

2. lava

B.

3. fireworks

C.

4. donkey

D.

5. compass

E.

READING WORDS

Circle the word that matches each picture.

1.
chest
chess
cheat

2.
sears
cheers
shears

3.
shell
shield
shed

4.
thed
threat
thread

5.
wet
wheat
what

6.
house
hows
hoss

7.
torsh
troch
torch

8.
bred
bread
bed

PREFIXES

Prefixes can be added before a word to change its meaning.

re means again	→	**re**view means to view again
dis means opposite of	→	**dis**appear means the opposite of appear
un (or in) means not	→	**un**opened means not opened
bi means two	→	a **bi**cycle is a cycle with two wheels
tri means three	→	a **tri**cycle is a cycle with three wheels

Underline the prefix. Draw a line to connect the word to its meaning.

1. respawn

A.

2. bicycle

B.

3. dislike

C.

4. tricycle

D.

5. unopened

E.

PREFIXES

Complete the crossword puzzle with the words below or their prefixes.

disagree	replay	unseen	incorrect
tripod	reappear	unclear	pretest
unable	tricycle	preschool	incomplete
redo	bicycle		

ACROSS

2   a cycle with three wheels

4   a test before a test

6   not complete

7   a prefix meaning the opposite of

8   not clear

10 to do again

11 a cycle with two wheels

13 not able

14 not seen

DOWN

1   to appear again

2   a stand with three legs

3   not correct

4   a school before school

5   to not agree

8   a prefix meaning not

9   to play again

11 a prefix meaning two

12 a prefix meaning to do again

SUFFIXES

Suffixes can be added at the end of a word to change its meaning.

Here's a play**ful** pig.

able means able to	→	enjoy**able** means able to be enjoyed
en means to make	→	dark**en** means to make dark
ful means full of	→	beauti**ful** means full of beauty
less means without	→	fear**less** means without fear

Add a suffix to the word below the blank to complete the sentence.

1. The _____ pig chases after the
              play

carrot on a stick.

2. Some potions will _____ mobs.
              weak

3. A _____ ghast will sometimes
         care

shoot itself.

4. Dying from a fall is _____ by
         avoid

carrying a bucket of water.

SUFFIXES

Suffixes can be added at the end of a word to change its meaning.

er is added to compare two

est is added to compare more than two

Creeper is tall.   This creeper is tall**er**.   This creeper is the tall**est**.

*Add **er** or **est** to complete each sentence.*

1. The diamond sword is the sharp_____ of all swords.

2. The ocelot is fast_____ than pig.

3. Wither is dark_____ than skeleton.

4. The Arctic Biome is the cold_____ biome.

5. Iron golem is the kind_____ mob in the village.

6. Horse's tail is long_____ than goat's tail.

SYLLABLES

Underline the vowel sounds in each word. Then circle the number of syllables. Hints: A syllable is a part of a word. Every syllable has a vowel sound.

1. melon

1 or 2

2. spider

1 or 2

3. sponge

1 or 2

4. fruit

1 or 2

5. moon

1 or 2

6. oven

1 or 2

7. cauldron

2 or 3

8. mooshroom

2 or 3

9. ocelot

2 or 3

DIVIDING SYLLABLES

Draw a line between the syllables of each word.
The first one is done for you.

I am not a ro/bot.

Hints:

- Divide between compound words.   **book/shelf**
- Prefixes and suffixes are syllables.   **creep/er**
- Divide after the long vowel.   **ro/bot**
- Divide after the consonant following a short vowel.   **Al/ex**

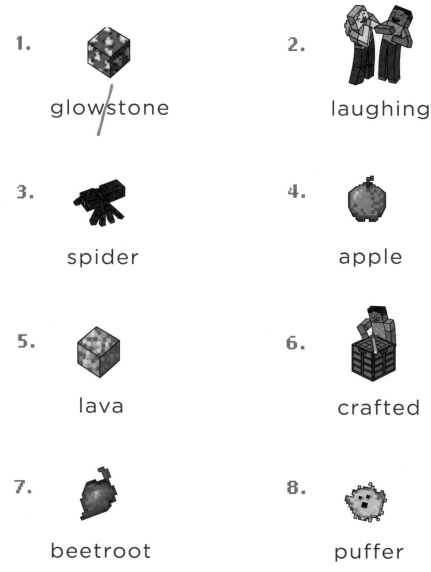

1. glow/stone

2. laughing

3. spider

4. apple

5. lava

6. crafted

7. beetroot

8. puffer

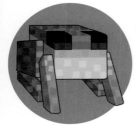

WHAT DOES IT MEAN?

Read each sentence. Use the context to figure out the meaning of the bolded word. Then circle the best meaning.

Hint: Sometimes clues to a word's meaning can be found in the picture.

1. The **shipwreck** was found in the deep ocean.

a sunken ship   a large new ship

2. Use the **enchanted** table to give weapons more power.

old   magical

3. Alex used the **shears** to get wool from sheep.

cutting tool   carrots

4. In **survival** mode, players must fight mobs to stay alive.

continuing to live   creating new building

LEARNING NEW WORDS

Complete the crossword puzzle using the words in the box.
Use a dictionary if needed.

hostile	provocative	crafting	mob
biome	passive	block	dungeon
retaliate	aggressive		

ACROSS

3   to get back at

6   a cube

7   dark, dank room under a building

9   ready to attack

10 unfriendly

DOWN

1   making

2   causing anger or excitement

4   short for mobile

5   a community with similar plants and animals

8   non-threatening

SUBJECT AND VERB

Connect the words to make a sentence. The first one is done for you.

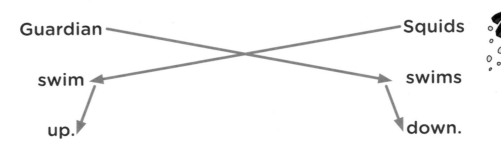

Guardian ————————→ Squids

swim ←———————— swims

up. ←——————— down.

1.   Horses   Steve

eat   eats

cake.   carrots.

2.   Alex   Baby zombies

ride   rides

a pig.   chickens.

3.   Creepers   Creeper

explodes   dance

to the music.   on the player.

SUBJECT AND VERB

Write the correct verb on the line.

1. Villagers _____ passive non-player characters.

   is / are

2. Baby villagers _____ adults after 20 minutes.

   become / becomes

3. A villager _____ clothes that show his job.

   wear / wears

4. Nitwits _____ not have jobs.

   do / does

5. Players _____ with villagers.

   trade / trades

6. Villagers _____ emeralds.

   like / likes

COLLECTIVE NOUNS

Write a collective noun to describe each group. Use a dictionary if needed.

A group of goats is called a **herd.**

bouquet   bale   family   flock   school

herd   swarm   pack   flight

1.

_____
of fish

2.

_____
of zombies

3.

_____
of flowers

4.

_____
of bees

5.

_____
of parrots

6.

_____
of stairs

7.

_____
of wolves

8.

_____
of hay

9.

_____
of mooshrooms

IRREGULAR PLURALS

*To make most nouns plural you add an **s**. But here are some tricky plurals you just need to learn. Draw a line from each noun to its plural.*

1. child

2. cactus

3. sheep

4. tooth

5. person

6. foot

A. feet

B. people

C. teeth

D. cacti

E. children

F. sheep

To form the past tense of most verbs, you add **ed**. But some words are different.

IT'S IN THE PAST

Complete each sentence with the correct past tense. Use a dictionary if needed.

grew	gave	ate	rode	swam

1. Iron golem (give)_____ the villager a flower.

2. Steve (ride)_____ the cart into the mine.

3. Squid (swim)_____ quickly away from the

guardian.

4. Horse (eat)_____ the carrot.

5. The flower (grow)_____ in the pot.

PAST TENSE

Complete the crossword puzzle with the correct past tense of each word. Use a dictionary if needed.

Dragon *flew* into a cobweb.

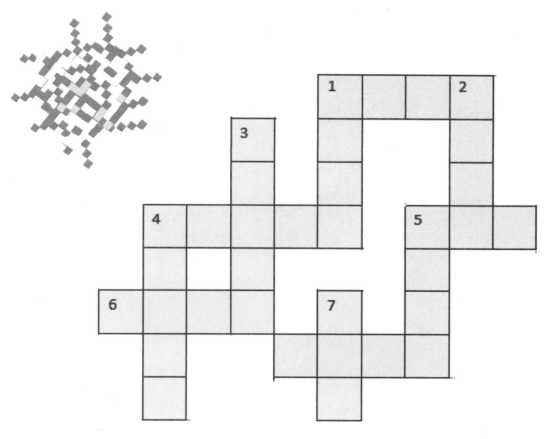

ACROSS

1 ring

4 stand

5 meet

6 ride

8 come

DOWN

1 read

2 give

3 write

4 shake

5 make

7 see

ADJECTIVES ON THE FARM

Choose an adjective to finish each sentence. Then underline the word that the adjective describes.

| spotted | red | white | noisy | hungry | furry | beautiful |

1. The farm mobs lived in the _____ barn.

2. The _____ cow mooed loudly.

3. The _____ cat sat on the fence.

4. The _____ horse wanted some hay.

5. The _____ butterfly floated around the farm.

6. The _____ cat chased the rabbit.

7. The _____ rabbit hopped away.

ADVERBS ON THE FARM

Choose an adverb to finish each sentence. Then underline the word that the adverb describes.

quickly	slowly	gently	patiently
loudly		aimlessly	sleepily

1. Pig oinked _____.

2. The chickens walked _____ around the farm.

3. Alex petted the pig _____.

4. Rabbit hopped _____ to get away from the cat.

5. The spotted cat sat _____ on the fence.

6. The clouds floated _____ across the sky.

7. The horse waited _____ for the hay.

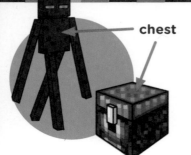

chest

MULTIPLE MEANING WORDS

Some words have more than one meaning. Draw lines from each multiple meaning word to its meanings.

an insect

a solid cube

a flying mammal

the sound of a bell

an animal that quacks

to go below the water

the outer layer of a tree

an animal enclosure

1. bat

2. pen

3. ring

4. fly

5. bark

6. block

7. sink

8. duck

to move out of the way

a basin for water

a circular band

a tool to write

to travel in the sky

a stick used to hit a ball

to keep from passing

the sound a dog makes

MULTIPLE MEANING WORDS

Read the sentence. Then write the letter of the meaning that matches the bold word.

1. If Steve is not careful, he will **trip** and fall into the lava. _____

    A. to stumble   B. a vacation

2. The diamond ore block is very **hard**. _____

    A. difficult   B. opposite of soft

3. The fireworks shot to the **right** of the building. _____

    A. correct   B. opposite of left

4. It is very **cold** in the Arctic Biome. _____

    A. a sickness   B. low temperature

5. It is **hard** to capture a creeper. _____

    A. difficult   B. opposite of soft

6. Steve hurt his **foot** when he kicked the block. _____

    A. a part of the body   B. 12 inches

pretty beautiful

SYNONYMS

Synonyms are words with the same meaning. Draw a line to match the synonyms.

1. scared   **A.** nice

2. delicious   **B.** courageous

3. shout   **C.** unhappy

4. kind   **D.** cruel

5. mean   **E.** afraid

6. smart   **F.** yell

7. sad   **G.** tasty

8. brave   **H.** clever

ANTONYMS

Antonyms are words with opposite meanings. Complete each sentence using an antonym of the bold word.

short   tall

| fast | cold | closed | happy | harm |

1. Alex **opened** the chest, then _____ it.

2. Skeleton is **sad**, but Steve is _____ .

3. A pig is **slow**, but a cat is _____ .

4. Some potions **heal** and some potions _____ .

5. The Desert Biome is **hot**, but the Arctic Biome is _____ .

CAPITALIZATION

Rewrite each sentence using correct capitalization.

Hints: Capitalize the first letter of:
- a sentence
- names
- days and months
- important words in a title

1. alex is a player in the minecraft world.

_____

2. steve wrote a book called <u>mindcraft mining</u>.

_____

3. in april, animals spawn lots of baby animals.

_____

4. on monday, creeper exploded.

_____

5. ender dragon flies around the end.

_____

IN THE DESERT

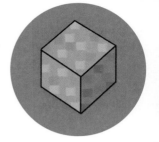

T
~~t~~he Desert Biome is made up of sandstone. it is very dry and

hot. very few plants and animals live in the desert. golden

rabbits can live there. cacti can live there, too. in some

deserts, there may be a desert temple. it is usually buried

in the ground. desert temples are dark. in the center of the

temple, there is a desert chest. it is filled with valuable loot. at

night, husks will spawn in the desert. many players avoid the

desert, but not steve. he likes to visit the desert in june when

it is really hot. sometimes alex will go with him. they have fun.

Sometimes they look for the desert chest.

POSSESSIVE NOUNS

Possessive nouns show ownership. Rewrite the phrase to show the possessive form. The first one is done for you.

Hints:

Singular nouns show possessives by adding an apostrophe and an *s*.   **the squid's ink**

Plural nouns show possessives by adding an apostrophe after the *s*.   **two creepers' explosion**

1. the sword that belongs to Steve   Steve's sword

2. the pig that belongs to Alex   _____

3. the eggs that belong to chickens   _____

4. the potions that belong to evokers   _____

5. the gems that belong to the villager   _____

6. the wings of a butterfly   _____

QUOTATION MARKS

Quotation marks enclose the words someone says. Place quotation marks around the words being said in the sentences below. The first one is done for you.

1. Steve asked, "Why wouldn't the skeleton go in the haunted house?"

2. I don't know, answered Alex.

3. Because it had no guts, said Steve. Alex and Steve laughed.

4. That's a funny riddle, laughed Alex. You are funny, Steve.

5. I have a lot more riddles, bragged Steve.

6. Alex rolled her eyes. I bet you do, she said.

ADDING DETAILS

Rewrite each sentence, adding details to make the sentence more interesting.

Adjectives
(describe people and things)

dark	heavy	enormous
creepy	tall	tiny
cute	strong	long	windy

Adverbs
(describe actions)

slowly	lazily
wildly	mightily
quickly	

Prepositional Phrases

under the trees	of heavy gems	over the mountain
by the river	down the mountain	in a cave

1. Some mountains have caves.

_____

2. The llama lives in the mountains.

_____

3. Llamas carry chests.

_____

4. Some rivers run.

_____

ADDING DETAILS

Add details to the sentences to tell how, when, and where.
Use words from the box or your own words.

How	When	Where
slowly	at night	in the jungle
loudly	after eating	in the Arctic
silently	early	by the cave
quickly	soon	in the ocean
sadly	always	over the city

1. The parrot squawks.

_____

2. The ship sank.

_____

3. The wolf jockey rode the wolf.

_____

4. The dragon flew.

_____

WRITING SENTENCES

Write a detailed sentence to tell about each picture. Use the words in the boxes to help you.

Nouns		Verbs	
Steve	wolf	exploded	tamed
creeper	Alex	crafted	held
pig	sword	spit	fight
llama	carrot	attacked	defended

1. _____

_____

2. _____

_____

3. _____

_____

4. _____

_____

WRITING AN OPINION

Who's the best villager—farmer, cleric, librarian, blacksmith, butcher, or nitwit? Fill in the blanks to write your opinion. Give three reasons for your opinion.

In my opinion, _____ is the best villager.
write the name of the villager

One reason is _____.
write a reason

Another reason is _____.
write another reason

The last reason is _____.
write another reason

That is why _____ is the best villager.
write the name of the villager

*A **fact** is something that can be proven true.*

WRITING TO INFORM

Think about a topic you know about or would like to learn about. Write to tell others about the topic. Use the outline to plan your writing.

Topic: _____

Introductory Sentence: _____

_____

Fact 1: _____

Detail: _____

Fact 2: _____

Detail: _____

Fact 3: _____

Detail: _____

Concluding Sentence: _____

_____

WRITING TO INFORM

Use the outline from page 36 to write about the topic.

_____

_____

_____

_____

_____

_____

_____

_____

_____

_____

_____

_____

_____

WRITING A STORY

Use the characters and setting to write a story.

Characters

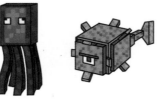

Setting

_____

_____

_____

_____

_____

_____

_____

_____

_____

_____

_____

WRITING A STORY

Use the characters, items, and setting pictured to write a story. If you run out of space here, use another sheet of paper or the computer to finish your story.

Characters and Items

Setting

_____

_____

_____

_____

_____

_____

_____

_____

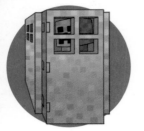

SEQUENCING

Read about how to tame a creeper. Then number the steps in the correct order.

How to Tame a Creeper

Do you want to tame a creeper? First, get him to come to your creeper trap. He won't be happy in the trap. But that's okay. Just let him settle down. Put one red flower on one corner of the trap. Then put one yellow flower by the opposite corner of the trap. Then open the trap. The creeper will follow you. It won't explode or harm you. You now have a tamed creeper.

_____ You now have a tamed creeper.

_____ Open the trap.

_____ Let the creeper settle down.

_____ Put a yellow flower on the opposite corner of the trap.

_____ Get the creeper to come into the trap.

_____ Put a red flower on one corner of the trap.

_____ The creeper will follow you.

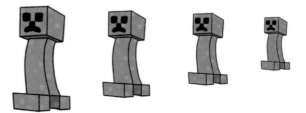

SEQUENCING

Read about how to build a snow golem. Then number the steps in the correct order.

How to Build a Snow Golem

Brr! It's cold outside. Let's build a snow golem. First, you'll need a shovel, some snow, a crafting table, and a pumpkin head. Punch the snow with your shovel to make eight snowballs. Put two snowballs in each of the two bottom left squares of the crafting table. Then put two snowballs in each of the two middle left squares of the crafting table. This will make two snow blocks. Then put the pumpkin on top for the head. Snow golem is great at throwing snowballs at your enemy.

_____ Punch the snow with your shovel to make eight snowballs.

_____ Now you have two snow blocks.

_____ Then put two snowballs in each of the two middle left squares of the crafting table.

_____ First, you'll need a shovel, some snow, a crafting table, and a pumpkin head.

_____ Put a pumpkin on top for the head.

_____ Put two snowballs in each of the two bottom left squares of the crafting table.

41

LOGIC ON THE FARM

It is feeding time on the farm, but the animals are scattered everywhere. Read the clues to help Alex find each of the animals.

*Hint: Put an **X** in the box when you know an animal is not in a place. Put an **O** in the box when you know where an animal is.*

Cow and chicken were not in the pen.

Horse was near its favorite food.

Chicken was not inside a building.

	In the corn field	Behind the haystack	In the barn	In the pen
Cow				
Chicken				
Pig				
Horse				

ZOMBIE LOGIC

Zombies have gone wild! They are popping up in unusual places. Read the clues to determine where each zombie is. Remember: they are in unusual places.

Hint: Put an **X** in the box when you know a zombie is not in a place. Put an **O** in the box when you know where a zombie is.

Husk is all wet!

Wolf Jockey will ride to the End.

Drowned is not in the forest or the village.

Zombie Villager is in the trees.

	Hot Biome	Underwater	Nether	Forest	Village
Wolf Jockey					
Husk					
Zombie Pigman					
Zombie Villager					
Drowned					

Hint: *Cause* is the **why** something happens. *Effect* is **what** happens.

CAUSE AND EFFECT

Draw a line to match the cause with the effect.

1. If you hit a pig,

2. When creeper meets a player,

3. When snow golem sees a hostile mob,

4. When a mob is hit by a snowball,

5. If you kill a cow,

A. it throws snowballs.

B. it drops leather or beef.

C. it gets angry.

D. it runs away.

E. it explodes.

CAUSE AND EFFECT

Complete the missing parts of the chart to show cause and effect.

Cause	Effect
1. When planted, a melon seed will	
2.	it will lay eggs.
3. Put two diamonds and a stick on a crafting table to	
4.	a squid will drop an ink sac.
5. Iron golem gives a poppy to a villager	
6.	you can ride it.

45

COMPARE AND CONTRAST

Read about wither and wither skeleton. Then, use the Venn diagram to compare and contrast them.

Hints: Things that describe only wither go in the left circle.

Things that describe only wither skeleton go in the right circle.

Things that describe both wither and wither skeleton go in the middle.

Wither has three heads. Wither likes to shoot explosive skulls at players. It turns a player's heart black. When wither dies, it drops a nether star. Wither is immune to fire, lava, and drowning. Wither skeleton is an underworld skeleton. It will attack with its stone sword. It also will turn a player's heart black. When a wither skeleton dies, it may drop its sword, bones, or coal. It is immune to fire and lava.

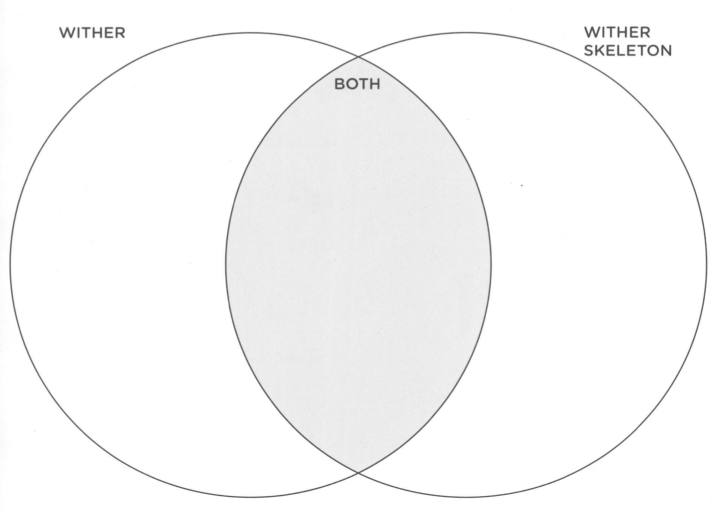

WITHER   WITHER
                                          SKELETON

BOTH

UNDERSTANDING PLACE VALUE

I don't need my calculator for these problems!

Use place value to solve the problems.

1. $5{,}000 + 600 + 30 + 3 =$ 5633

2. $2{,}000 + 60 + 1 =$ 2,061

3. $7{,}000 + 200 + 80 =$ 7,280

4. $3{,}000 + 400 + 90 + 1 =$ 3,491

5. $9{,}000 + 100 + 20 =$ 9,120

6. $8{,}000 + 500 + 70 + 6 =$ 8,576

7. $1{,}000 + 900 + 90 + 9 =$ 1,999

8. $4{,}000 + 3 =$ 4,0033

NUMBERS TO 1,000

Write the number that goes between.

1. 4,893 [| | |] 4,895

2. 5,000 [| | |] 5,002

3. 3,999 [| | |] 4,001

4. 6,821 [| | |] 6,823

5. 1,739 [| | |] 1,741

6. 7,013 [| | |] 7,015

7. 9,001 [| | |] 9,003

8. 8,220 [| | |] 8,222

EXPLODING NUMBERS

Creeper has been exploding some numbers. Use place value to write the missing numbers.

1. $2,496 = 2,000 +$ ⬡_____ $+ 90 + 6$

2. $6,052 =$ ⬡_____ $+ 50 + 2$

3. $7,913 = 7,000 + 900 + 10 +$ ⬡_____

4. $4,843 = 4,000 +$ ⬡_____ $+ 40 + 3$

5. $1,359 =$ ⬡_____ $+ 300 +$ ⬡_____ $+ 9$

6. $9,999 = 9,000 +$ ⬡_____ $+$ ⬡_____ $+ 9$

7. $3,001 =$ ⬡_____ $+$ ⬡_____

8. $2,834 =$ ⬡_____ $+$ ⬡_____ $+$ ⬡_____ $+$ ⬡_____

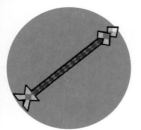

ADD TO 100

Draw each problem using lines for tens and dots for ones.
Then count and add. The first one is done for you.

$| = 10 \qquad \cdot = 1$

1.
$$\begin{array}{r} 33 \\ + 52 \\ \hline 85 \end{array}$$
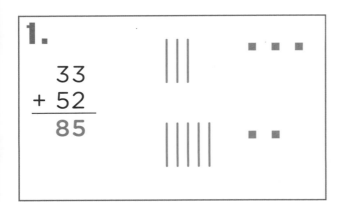

2.
$$\begin{array}{r} 40 \\ + 32 \\ \hline \end{array}$$

3.
$$\begin{array}{r} 17 \\ + 62 \\ \hline \end{array}$$

4.
$$\begin{array}{r} 54 \\ + 13 \\ \hline \end{array}$$

5.
$$\begin{array}{r} 43 \\ + 55 \\ \hline \end{array}$$

6.
$$\begin{array}{r} 24 \\ + 42 \\ \hline \end{array}$$

ADD TO 100

Solve each problem. Use the answers to solve the riddle.

1. 61
   + 27

2. 55
   + 32

3. 73
   + 26

4. 42
   + 23

O   T   R   F

5. 71
   + 26

6. 12
   + 51

7. 83
   + 10

8. 73
   + 25

B   M   S   C

9. 53
   + 33

10. 38
    + 51

11. 64
    + 15

12. 36
    + 41

V   H   I   E

Q: Why does witch like to stay in a hotel?

COPY THE LETTERS FROM THE ANSWERS ABOVE TO FIND OUT.

65   88   99   87   89   77   97   99   88   88   63

93   77   99   86   79   98   77

| = 10   • = 1

SUBTRACT WITHIN 100

Draw lines and dots to show the first number. Then cross out the second number. Count the amount that's left. The first one is done for you.

1.

   57
- 16
─────
   41

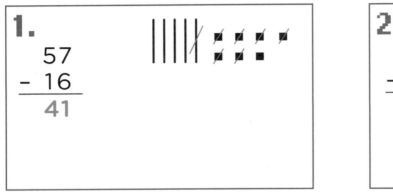

2.

   79
- 43

3.

   28
- 13

4.

   67
- 26

5.

   86
- 72

6.

   45
- 22

SUBTRACT WITHIN 100

Solve each problem. Use the answers to solve the riddle.

1. 77
  − 23

2. 56
  − 22

3. 49
  − 17

4. 67
  − 41

I   K   B   R

5. 99
  − 46

6. 43
  − 31

7. 65
  − 35

8. 77
  − 46

T   O   L   C

9. 98
  − 34

10. 47
  − 14

11. 59
  − 14

12. 85
  − 14

A   P   H   E

Q: How do you stop hostile mobs from attacking you?

COPY THE LETTERS FROM THE ANSWERS ABOVE TO FIND OUT.

32   30   12   31   34   53   45   71   54   26

33   64   53   45

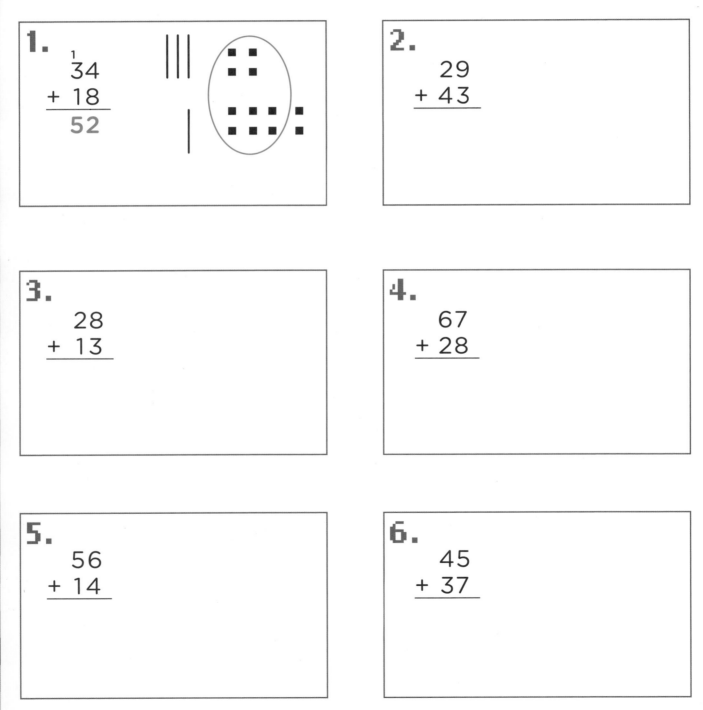

| = 10   • = 1

ADDITION WITH REGROUPING

Draw lines and dots to show the numbers. Then combine the ones. Regroup to make ten. Then combine the tens. The first one is done for you.

1.

$$\begin{array}{r} {\scriptstyle 1} \\ 34 \\ +\ 18 \\ \hline 52 \end{array}$$

2.

$$\begin{array}{r} 29 \\ +\ 43 \\ \hline \end{array}$$

3.

$$\begin{array}{r} 28 \\ +\ 13 \\ \hline \end{array}$$

4.

$$\begin{array}{r} 67 \\ +\ 28 \\ \hline \end{array}$$

5.

$$\begin{array}{r} 56 \\ +\ 14 \\ \hline \end{array}$$

6.

$$\begin{array}{r} 45 \\ +\ 37 \\ \hline \end{array}$$

ADDITION WITH REGROUPING

Solve the problems. Use the answers to solve the riddle.

1. 36 + 24	2. 49 + 37	3. 65 + 18	4. 52 + 49
A	K	B	T

5. 68 + 27	6. 39 + 46	7. 87 + 18	8. 71 + 39
U	I	E	H

9. 45 + 26	10. 17 + 64	11. 55 + 29	12. 25 + 47
S	C	N	L

Q: Why is squid always giggling?

COPY THE LETTERS FROM THE ANSWERS ABOVE TO FIND OUT.

83 105 81 60 95 71 105   85 91 110 60 71

—

101 105 84   101 85 81 86 72 105 71

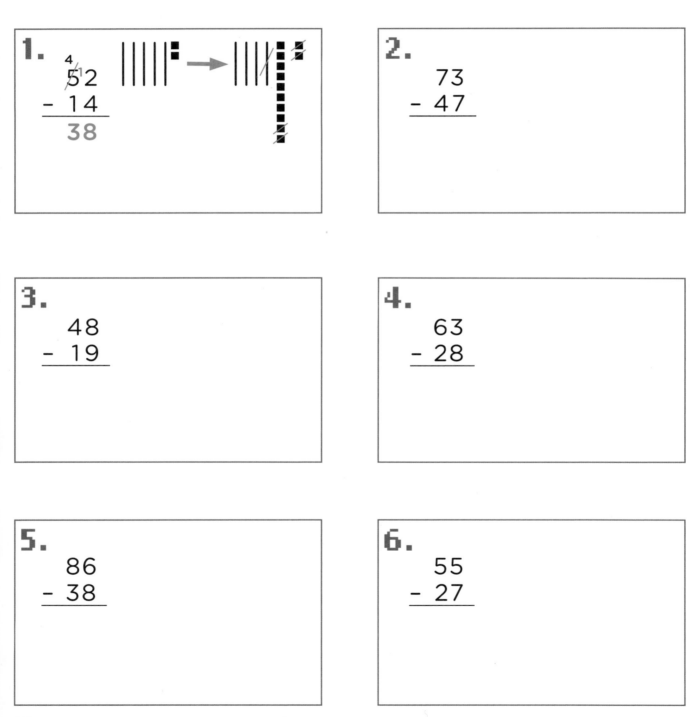

SUBTRACTION WITH REGROUPING

| = 10   • = 1

Draw lines and dots to show the first number. Regroup a ten into ten ones. Then cross out the second number. Count the amount that's left. The first one is done for you.

1.
```
   4
   5̸1
   5 2
 - 1 4
 ─────
   3 8
```

2.
```
   7 3
 - 4 7
```

3.
```
   4 8
 - 1 9
```

4.
```
   6 3
 - 2 8
```

5.
```
   8 6
 - 3 8
```

6.
```
   5 5
 - 2 7
```

SUBTRACTION WITH REGROUPING

Solve the problems. Use the answers to solve the riddle.

1. 83
− 29

A

2. 76
− 38

P

3. 41
− 27

B

4. 80
− 45

T

5. 74
− 26

O

6. 52
− 37

E

7. 91
− 54

S

8. 70
− 24

P

9. 55
− 29

H

Q: Where does sheep go to be sheared?

COPY THE LETTERS FROM THE ANSWERS ABOVE TO FIND OUT.

35   48   35   26   15   14   54   54

14   54   54   37   26   48   46

MATH IN THE DESERT

Read and solve each problem. Use the box to show how you solved the problem.

1. The desert had 37 dead bushes and 15 cacti. How many plants were in the desert?

_____

2. One llama spawned 17 baby llamas. Another llama spawned 28 baby llamas. How many baby llamas were there?

_____

3. There were 52 baby llamas wandering in the desert, and 37 of them became adult llamas. How many baby llamas were left?

_____

4. Husk found two chests. The first chest was filled with 46 diamonds and the other was filled with 39 diamonds. How many more diamonds were in the first chest than in the second chest?

_____

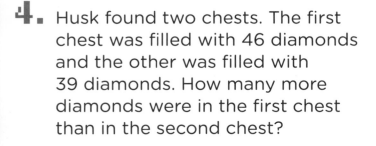

MATH IN THE MINES

Read and solve each problem. Use the box to show how you solved the problem.

1. Steve found 57 gems in the mine. He loaded 38 of the gems in the cart. How many gems were left in the mine?

_____

2. Steve found 75 emeralds and 27 diamonds. How many gems did he find in all?

_____

3. Alex found 46 diamonds and Steve found 27 diamonds. How many more diamonds did Alex find than Steve found?

_____

4. Alex found 46 diamonds and she found some emeralds too. She found 18 more diamonds than emeralds. How many emeralds did she find?

_____

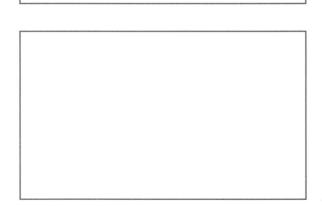

Yikes! These mobs are multiplying!

MULTIPLYING MOBS

Read the problem. Draw a picture to solve.

1. Eight spiders were climbing up the wall. Each spider has 8 legs. How many spider legs are there in all?

_____ spider legs

2. Nine groups of zombie villagers were sitting in groups of 3. How many zombie villagers are there all together?

_____ zombie villagers

3. The skeletons were marching in a line. There were 7 rows of skeletons with 6 skeletons in each row. How many skeletons were marching?

_____ skeletons

4. Creepers were hiding behind the trees. There were 8 trees and 4 creepers behind each tree. How many creepers were hiding?

_____ creepers

MULTIPLICATION ARRAYS

Write multiplication equations to tell how many blocks are in each wall of redstone. The first one is done for you.

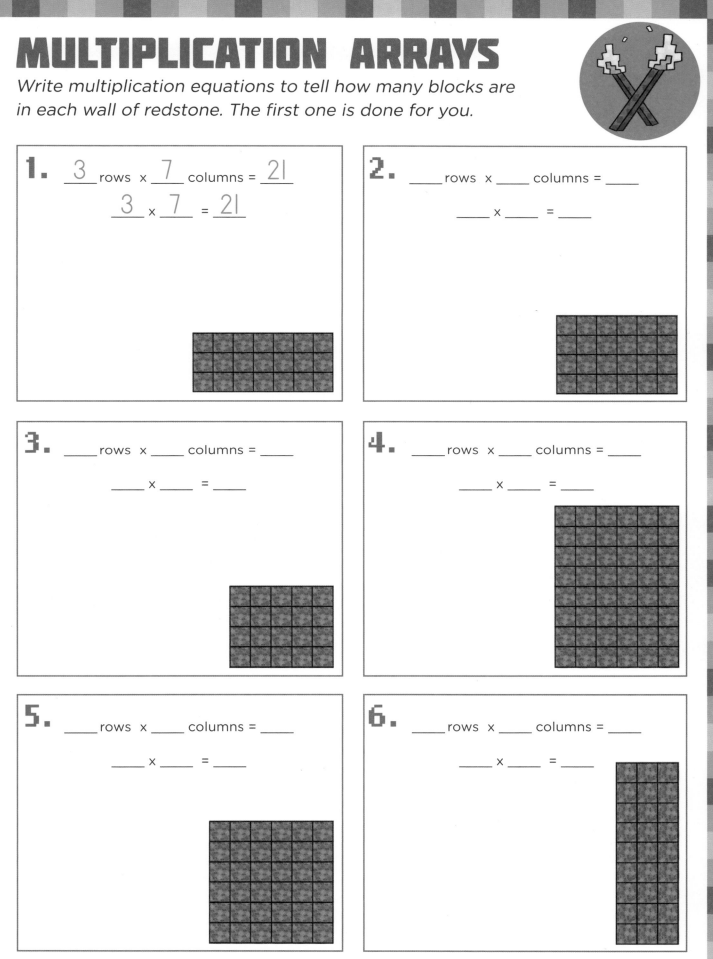

1. __3__ rows x __7__ columns = __21__

__3__ x __7__ = __21__

2. ____ rows x ____ columns = ____

____ x ____ = ____

3. ____ rows x ____ columns = ____

____ x ____ = ____

4. ____ rows x ____ columns = ____

____ x ____ = ____

5. ____ rows x ____ columns = ____

____ x ____ = ____

6. ____ rows x ____ columns = ____

____ x ____ = ____

MULTIPLICATION CHART

Complete the multiplication chart.

x	0	1	2	3	4	5	6	7	8	9	10
0	0										
1					4						
2											20
3				9							
4									32		
5						25					
6											
7		7									
8											
9				27							
10											100

MULTIPLICATION FACTS

Solve the problems. Use the key to color the orb.

| 8, 9, 10 | 12 | 14, 15, 16 | 18, 21, 25 | 4, 6, 20 | 5, 27, 28, 30, 32, 56 | 35, 36, 42, 49, 54, 64, 72, 81 |

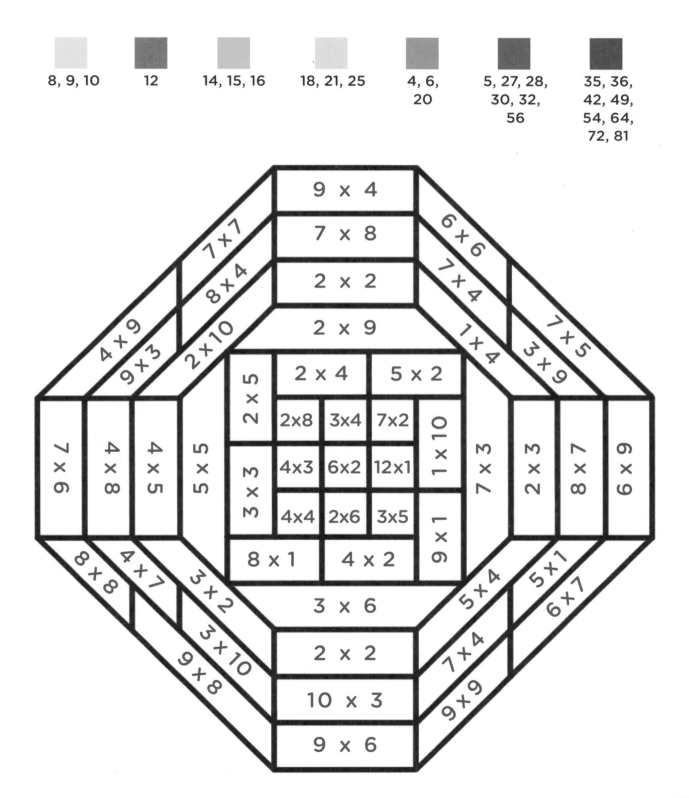

MULTIPLYING BY TEN

Multiply by ten. Find the pattern.

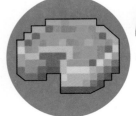

Multiplying by ten is
as easy as pie!

1. 1 x 10 = _____

2. 2 x 10 = _____

3. 3 x 10 = _____

4. 4 x 10 = _____

5. 5 x 10 = _____

6. 6 x 10 = _____

7. 7 x 10 = _____

8. 8 x 10 = _____

9. 9 x 10 = _____

10. 10 x 10 = _____

11. 11 x 10 = _____

12. 12 x 10 = _____

What's the pattern?

_____

_____

MULTIPLYING BY TENS

Multiply by tens to solve the problems.

Hint: 3 x 4 = 12   3 x 40 = 120

1. 2 x 50 = _____

2. 6 x 40 = _____

3. 30 x 7 = _____

4. 60 x 6 = _____

5. 70 x 2 = _____

6. 4 x 80 = _____

7. 5 x 40 = _____

8. 3 x 90 = _____

9. 60 x 5 = _____

10. 4 x 70 = _____

11. 20 x 4 = _____

12. 50 x 6 = _____

13. 4 x 40 = _____

14. 3 x 50 = _____

15. 7 x 50 = _____

16. 20 x 6 = _____

This is like three problems in one!

MULTIPLYING WITHIN 100

Solve the problems. The first two are done for you.

43	Multiply the ones.	Multiply the tens.	Add.
x 2	$3 \times 2 = 6$	$40 \times 2 = 80$	$80 + 6 = 86$
86			

1. 24
x2
8
+40
48

2. 46
x2
12
+80
92

3. 63
x3

4. 51
x4

5. 36
x5

6. 27
x6

7. 54
x4

8. 64
x6

9. 25
x5

10. 31
x7

11. 82
x7

12. 74
x3

MULTIPLYING WITHIN 100

Solve the problems. Use the answer to solve the riddle.

1. 54 x 6	2. 26 x 5	3. 42 x 7	4. 73 x 5	5. 61 x 8
U	H	R	A	S

6. 38 x 6	7. 24 x 3	8. 45 x 2	9. 56 x 4	10. 62 x 5
O	C	D	T	N

11. 93 x 7	12. 44 x 5	13. 37 x 3	14. 43 x 7
L	E	K	B

Q: How does Steve stay in shape?

COPY THE LETTERS FROM THE ANSWERS ABOVE TO FIND OUT.

___ ___   ___ ___ ___ ___   ___ ___ ___ ___ ___ ___
130 220   294 324 310 488   365 294 228 324 310 90

___ ___ ___   ___ ___ ___ ___ ___ .
224 130 220   301 651 228 72 111

DIVISION

Solve the problems.

1. The chickens laid 20 eggs. There are 5 chickens. They each laid the same number of eggs. How many eggs did each chicken lay?

20 ÷ 5 = _____

2. Steve saw 12 wither heads peeking out from behind the tree. He knows that each wither has 3 heads. How many withers were in the tree?

12 ÷ 3 = _____

3. Steve needs 24 melon seeds. Each melon has 4 seeds. How many melons will Steve need?

24 ÷ 4 = _____

4. Witch had 21 potions. She had a case with 3 shelves. She put the same number of potions on each shelf. How many potions were on each shelf?

21 ÷ 3 = _____

DIGGING DIVISION

Read the problem and look at the picture.
Solve the problem.

1. Steve found 48 diamonds in the mine. He piled them into 6 piles. How many diamonds were in each pile?

48 ÷ 6 = _____

2. Steve had 27 emeralds and 3 chests. He put the same number of emeralds in each chest. How many emeralds were in each chest?

27 ÷ 3 = _____

3. Steve had 36 tin ingots. He stacked the ingots into 4 equal stacks. How many ingots were in each stack?

36 ÷ 4 = _____

4. Steve had 18 gold ingots. He stacked the gold ingots into 3 equal stacks. How many gold ingots were in each stack?

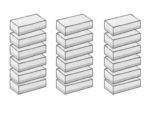

18 ÷ 3 = _____

FACT FAMILIES

Look at the fact families. Then fill in the missing numbers.

1.

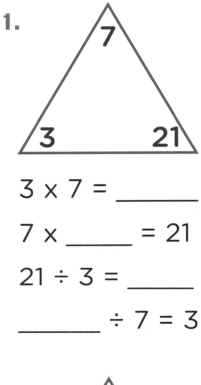

$3 \times 7 = $ _____

$7 \times $ _____ $= 21$

$21 \div 3 = $ _____

_____ $\div 7 = 3$

2.

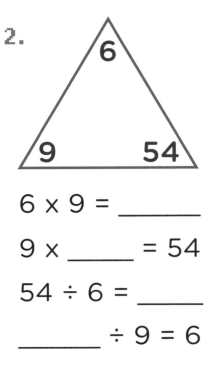

$6 \times 9 = $ _____

$9 \times $ _____ $= 54$

$54 \div 6 = $ _____

_____ $\div 9 = 6$

3.

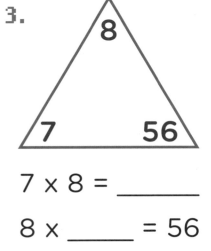

$7 \times 8 = $ _____

$8 \times $ _____ $= 56$

$56 \div 7 = $ _____

_____ $\div 8 = 7$

4.

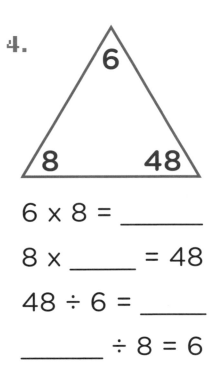

$6 \times 8 = $ _____

$8 \times $ _____ $= 48$

$48 \div 6 = $ _____

_____ $\div 8 = 6$

DIVISION FACTS

Complete each equation.

1. $3 \times 4 = \underline{\hspace{2cm}}$ $12 \div 3 = \underline{\hspace{2cm}}$ $12 \div 4 = \underline{\hspace{2cm}}$

2. $7 \times 6 = \underline{\hspace{2cm}}$ $42 \div 6 = \underline{\hspace{2cm}}$ $42 \div 7 = \underline{\hspace{2cm}}$

3. $8 \times 5 = \underline{\hspace{2cm}}$ $40 \div 8 = \underline{\hspace{2cm}}$ $40 \div 5 = \underline{\hspace{2cm}}$

4. $9 \times 4 = \underline{\hspace{2cm}}$ $36 \div 9 = \underline{\hspace{2cm}}$ $36 \div 4 = \underline{\hspace{2cm}}$

5. $7 \times 5 = \underline{\hspace{2cm}}$ $35 \div 7 = \underline{\hspace{2cm}}$ $35 \div 5 = \underline{\hspace{2cm}}$

6. $5 \times 9 = \underline{\hspace{2cm}}$ $45 \div 5 = \underline{\hspace{2cm}}$ $45 \div 9 = \underline{\hspace{2cm}}$

7. $4 \times 6 = \underline{\hspace{2cm}}$ $24 \div 4 = \underline{\hspace{2cm}}$ $24 \div 6 = \underline{\hspace{2cm}}$

8. $9 \times 7 = \underline{\hspace{2cm}}$ $63 \div 9 = \underline{\hspace{2cm}}$ $63 \div 7 = \underline{\hspace{2cm}}$

DIVIDING BY TENS

Complete each equation.

1. $36 \div 9 = 4$

$360 \div 9 =$ _____

$360 \div 90 =$ _____

2. $64 \div 8 = 8$

$640 \div 8 =$ _____

$640 \div 80 =$ _____

3. $27 \div 9 = 3$

$270 \div 9 =$ _____

$270 \div 30 =$ _____

4. $42 \div 7 = 6$

$420 \div 7 =$ _____

$420 \div 70 =$ _____

5. $54 \div 9 = 6$

$540 \div 9 =$ _____

$540 \div 90 =$ _____

6. $49 \div 7 = 7$

$490 \div 7 =$ _____

$490 \div 70 =$ _____

7. $45 \div 5 = 9$

$450 \div 5 =$ _____

$450 \div 50 =$ _____

8. $56 \div 8 = 7$

$560 \div 8 =$ _____

$560 \div 80 =$ _____

9. $32 \div 4 = 8$

$320 \div 4 =$ _____

$320 \div 40 =$ _____

DIVISION

Solve the division problems. The first one is done for you.

1.

$$9\overline{)54}$$ with quotient 6

2.

$$8\overline{)72}$$

3.

$$6\overline{)36}$$

4.

$$8\overline{)32}$$

5.

$$4\overline{)24}$$

6.

$$2\overline{)18}$$

7.

$$7\overline{)21}$$

8.

$$5\overline{)35}$$

9.

$$8\overline{)64}$$

10.

$$9\overline{)63}$$

11.

$$6\overline{)54}$$

12.

$$9\overline{)27}$$

5 R2   Show
5)27   what's
-25   left over
2   using R.

DIVIDING WITH REMAINDERS

Solve the division problems.

1.

7)58

2.

6)42

3.

9)75

4.

4)26

5.

4)37

6.

9)85

7.

8)61

8.

7)43

9.

8)68

10.

6)22

11.

8)27

12.

8)55

DIVIDING WITHIN 100

Solve the division problems. Then use the answers to solve the riddle.

1.

$7\overline{)59}$

W

2.

$5\overline{)28}$

S

3.

$9\overline{)87}$

A

4.

$6\overline{)46}$

E

5.

$8\overline{)56}$

T

6.

$7\overline{)33}$

P

7.

$9\overline{)57}$

H

8.

$7\overline{)68}$

O

9.

$9\overline{)58}$

N

Q: Where can you sell Minecraft eggs?

COPY THE LETTERS FROM THE ANSWERS ABOVE TO FIND OUT.

9 R6   9   7   6 R3 7 R4   5 R3 4 R5 9 R6 8 R3 6 R4

5 R3 6 R3 9 R5 4 R5 .

CRAFTING PROBLEMS

Look at the crafting recipes. Answer the questions.

diamond   diamond   stick   diamond   diamond   diamond
        block   axe   shovel   sword

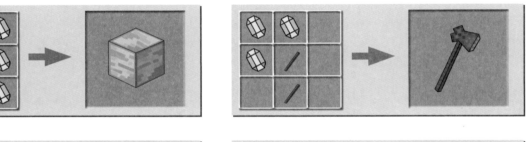

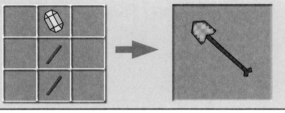 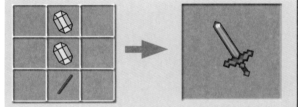

1. Steve has 63 diamonds. How many diamond blocks can he craft? _____

2. Steve wants to craft 8 diamond swords. How many diamonds and sticks does he need? _____

3. Steve has 26 diamonds. How many diamond axes can he craft? _____

4. Steve wants to craft 5 diamond axes, 4 diamond shovels, and 6 diamond swords. How many diamonds and sticks will he need? _____

CRAFTING DIAMOND ARMOR

Look at the crafting recipes. Answer the questions.

diamond   diamond helmet   diamond chest plate   diamond leggings   diamond boots

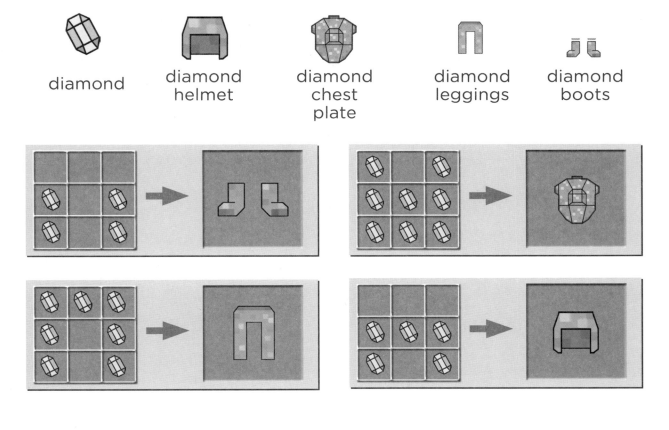

1. Steve is crafting 8 diamond suits of armor. Write multiplication problems to show how many diamonds he will need to craft the helmets, chest plates, leggings, and boots he will need.

2. Steve has 40 diamonds. Write division problems to show how many of each armor item he could craft.

77

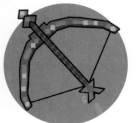

COUNTING DOLLARS AND COINS

Add up the value of each group of dollars and coins.
Write the amount on the line.

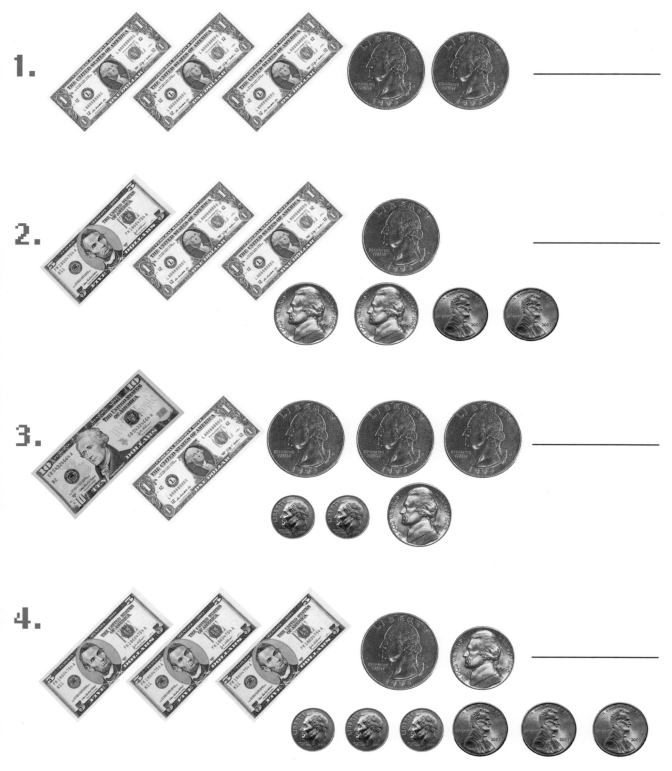

1. _____

2. _____

3. _____

4. _____

MINECRAFTER'S CAFE

Steve has $10.00 each week to spend on school lunches. Look at the menu and decide how Steve will spend his money and how much he will have left over.

Beef Plate
$2.50

Drumstick Plate
$2.00

Porkchop Plate
$2.25

Rabbit Stew
$1.50

	Lunch	Paid	Subtract from $10
Monday			
Tuesday			
Wednesday			
Thursday			
Friday			

UNDERSTANDING VALUE

Look at the value of gold. Answer the questions.

gold block

gold ingot

gold nugget

1. Which is worth more: a gold block or a gold ingot?

   _____

2. Which is worth more: a gold nugget or a gold ingot?

   _____

3. Alex has 5 gold blocks. How many gold ingots can she craft?

   _____

4. Alex wants to craft 2 gold blocks. How many gold nuggets will she need?   _____

UNDERSTANDING VALUE

Look at the crafting tables. Then answer the questions and help Alex craft some gold tools.

stick · gold ingot · gold pickaxe · gold shovel · gold hoe

1. Alex has 3 gold ingots and 2 sticks. What tool can she craft?

_____

2. Alex wants to craft 2 gold pickaxes, 3 gold shovels, and 1 gold hoe. How many gold ingots and sticks will she need?

_____

3. Alex has 6 gold ingots and 6 sticks. She could craft 1 gold pickaxe, 1 gold shovel, and 1 gold hoe. Write 2 other combinations of tools she could craft.

_____

TWO-DIMENSIONAL SHAPES

Read the clues. Then draw the shape and name it.

triangle   rhombus   rectangle   circle   square   hexagon   pentagon   octagon

1.

0 sides
0 angles

2.

4 sides
4 right angles
all sides same length

3.

4 sides
no right angles

4.

3 sides
3 angles

5.

5 sides
5 angles

6.

4 sides
4 right angles
2 sets of sides the same length

7.

8 sides
8 angles

8.

6 sides
6 angles

THREE-DIMENSIONAL SHAPES

Draw a line from each three-dimensional shape to its name.

1.

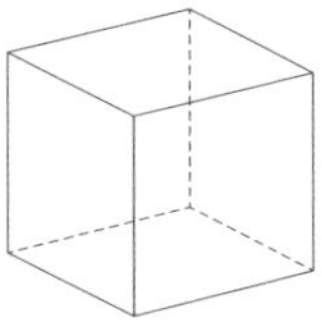

2.

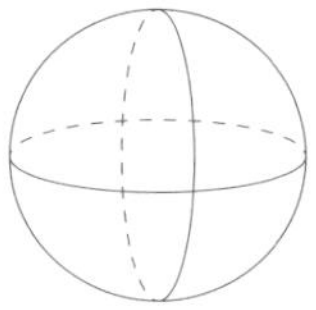

3.

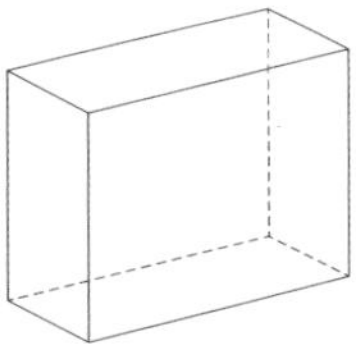

4.

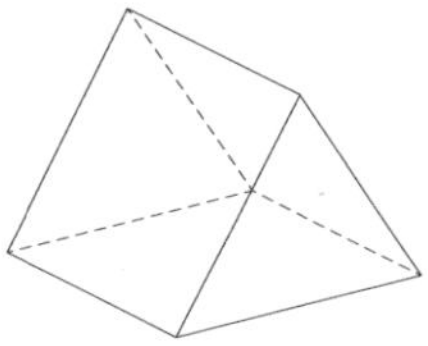

5.

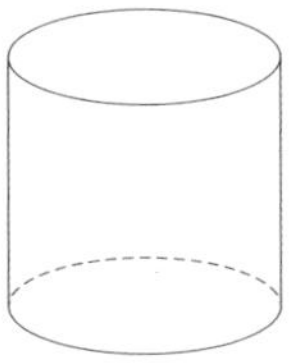

6.

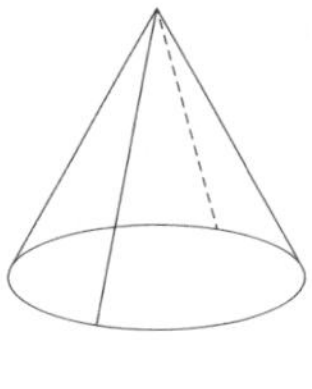

A. rectangular prism

B. cone

C. triangular prism

D. sphere

E. cylinder

F. cube

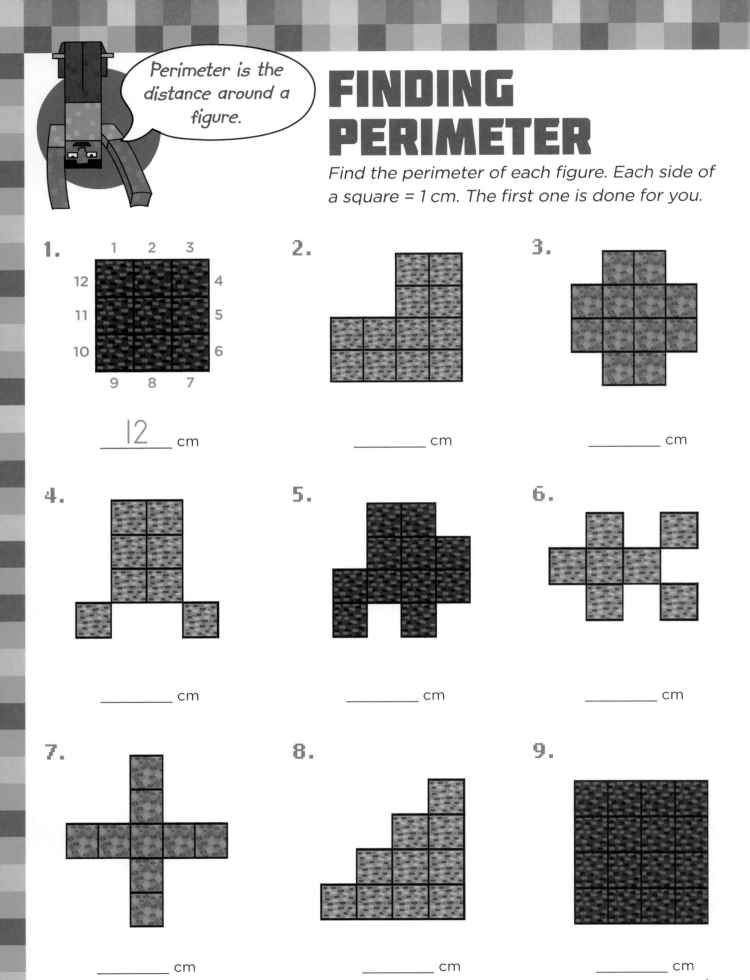

Perimeter is the distance around a figure.

FINDING PERIMETER

Find the perimeter of each figure. Each side of a square = 1 cm. The first one is done for you.

1.

	1	2	3	
12				4
11				5
10				6
	9	8	7	

_12_ cm

2.

_____ cm

3.

_____ cm

4.

_____ cm

5.

_____ cm

6.

_____ cm

7.

_____ cm

8.

_____ cm

9.

_____ cm

84

FINDING AREA

Find the area of each square.

1.

_____ cm

2.

_____ cm

3.

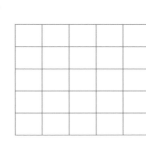

_____ cm

4.

_____ cm

5.

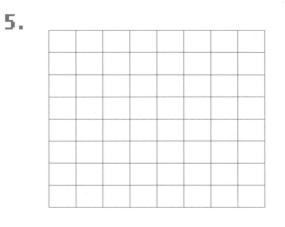

_____ cm

6.

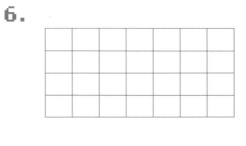

_____ cm

7.

_____ cm

8.

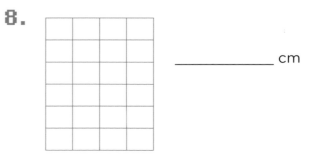

_____ cm

Let's make 3 equal shares!

FRACTIONS

Write a fraction to tell about the shaded area.
The first one is done for you.

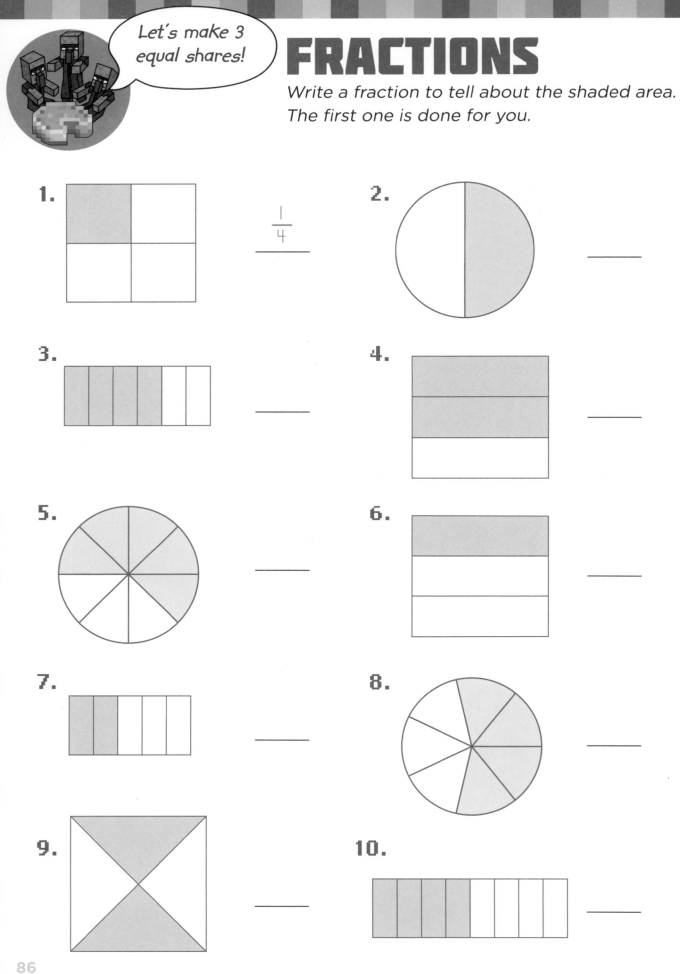

1. $\frac{1}{4}$

2. _____

3. _____

4. _____

5. _____

6. _____

7. _____

8. _____

9. _____

10. _____

FRACTIONS

Color each shape to match the fraction. The first one is done for you.

1. 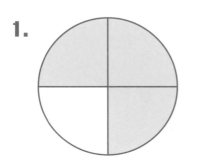 $\dfrac{3}{4}$

2. 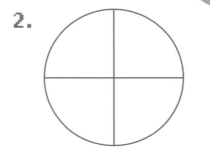 $\dfrac{2}{4}$

3. 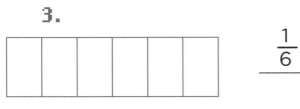 $\dfrac{1}{6}$

4. 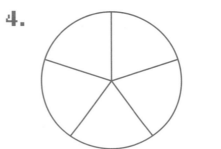 $\dfrac{3}{5}$

5. 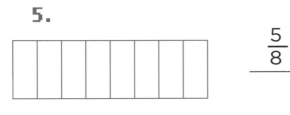 $\dfrac{5}{8}$

6. 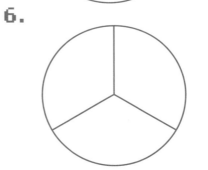 $\dfrac{2}{3}$

7. 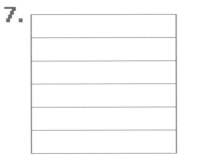 $\dfrac{5}{6}$

8. 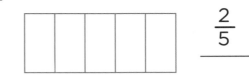 $\dfrac{2}{5}$

9. 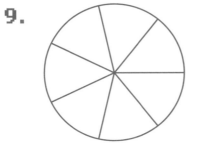 $\dfrac{5}{7}$

10. 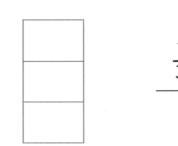 $\dfrac{1}{3}$

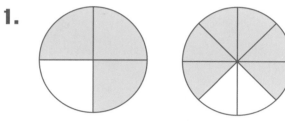

I want two-eighths of a pie instead of one-fourth because 2 is more than 1.

EQUIVALENT FRACTIONS

Color and write an equivalent fraction. The first one is done for you.

1.

$$\frac{3}{4} = \frac{6}{8}$$

2.

$$\frac{2}{3} = \frac{}{6}$$

3.

$$\frac{1}{2} = \frac{}{8}$$

4.

$$\frac{1}{4} = \frac{}{12}$$

5.

$$\frac{4}{6} = \frac{}{3}$$

6.

$$\frac{4}{16} = \frac{}{8}$$

7. Explain nitwit's mistake in his pie request.

_____

_____

HUMAN BODY

Label the organs of the human body.

Inside the human body is very interesting.

brain   large intestines   lungs   stomach   vein

heart   small intestines   liver   artery

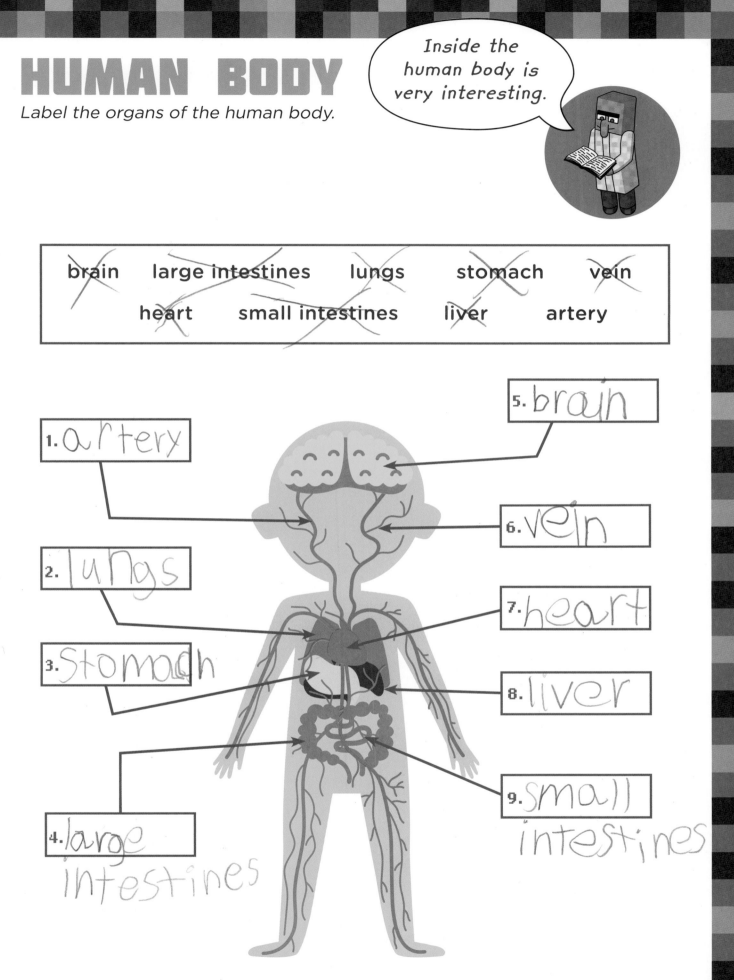

5. brain

1. artery

2. lungs

3. Stomach

4. large intestines

6. vein

7. heart

8. liver

9. small intestines

THE EYE

Read about the eye. Then label its parts.

The **cornea** is the outer covering of the eye. It protects the **pupil**. The black circle in the middle of the eye is the pupil. It is a small hole that lets light come into the eye. The **lens** is behind the pupil. It sends the light to the back of the eye. The **retina** changes the light into nerve signals. The **optic nerve** carries images to the brain.

pupil	lens	retina
cornea	optic nerve	

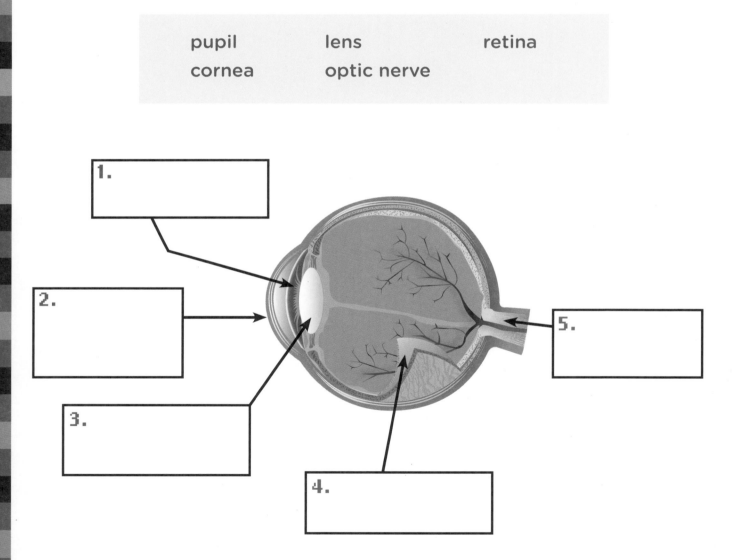

1.

2.

3.

4.

5.

THE EAR

Read about the ear and how it hears.
Answer the questions.

I like my ears!

Your **outer ear** collects sound. Sound moves through the **ear canal** in sound waves. The **middle ear** takes in the sound waves. The sound waves hit the **eardrum**, which begins to vibrate. The vibrations move to the **inner ear**. The nerves in the inner ear send signals to the brain. The brain takes in the information.

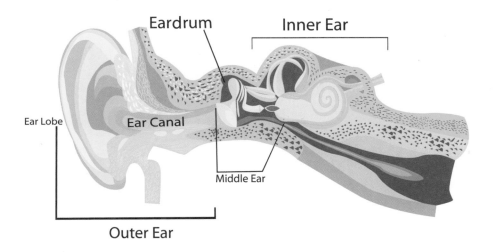

1. Where does sound enter the ear? _____

2. How does sound move through the ear canal? _____

_____

3. What happens when sound waves hit the eardrum? _____

_____

4. What part of the inner ear sends signals to the brain? _____

_____

When you know your eggs, you know what to expect is inside.

INHERITED TRAITS

Read about traits. Draw a line from each mob to its offspring.

All living things get traits from their parents. Some traits are eye color, hair color, skin color, and height. Every living thing has many different traits. Traits from parents are called **inherited traits**.

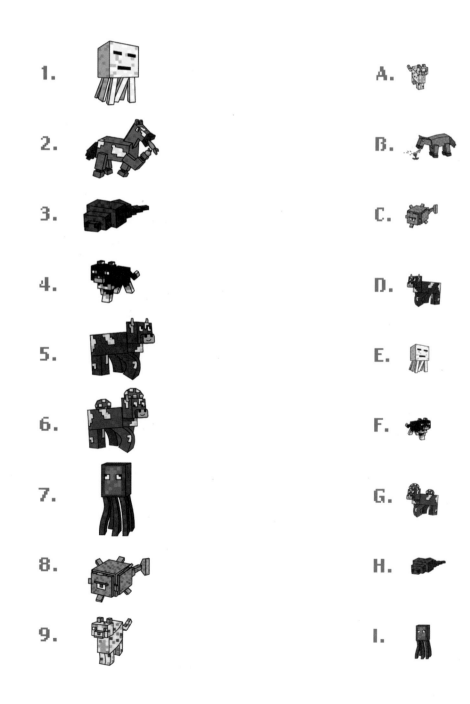

1.

2.

3.

4.

5.

6.

7.

8.

9.

A.

B.

C.

D.

E.

F.

G.

H.

I.

INHERITED TRAITS

I think he has your eyes.

You get your traits from your parents. But even children who have the same parents look different. And children who don't live with their birth parents may look completely different from their parents. Compare yourself to an adult who you live with. Circle the answer that best describes you and the adult.

Trait	You	Adult
eye color	brown blue hazel green	brown blue hazel green
hair color	brown blond black red	brown blond black red
hair texture	thick thin straight curly	thick thin straight curly
freckles	yes no	yes no
dimples	yes no	yes no

1. How are you and the adult alike? _____

_____

_____

2. How are you different from the adult? _____

_____

_____

3. Who do you get most of your traits from? _____

_____

_____

ANIMALS/MAMMALS

Read about mammals. Cross out the animals that are not mammals. Then find the mammal names in the puzzle.

Mammals are a group of animals with similar characteristics. In the real world, mammals have lungs and breathe air. They are covered with hair or fur. The females give birth to their babies and supply the babies with milk to drink.

cat	butterfly	wolf	rabbit
donkey	pig	squid	spider
chicken	cow	ocelot	
horse	llama	sheep	

R D O N K E Y N W
N W D O F X E O R
R G R L C K C P J
P A O Z C E A D H
E W B I M M L O P
E P H B A R R O X
H C T L I S P B T
S R L A E T I J P
B B P L C D G J T

ANIMALS/FISH

Read about fish. Then label parts of the fish.

Guardian is a Minecraft mob that lives in water. In the real world, fish live in the water too. Fish have gills that allow them to breathe underwater. They also have backbones, scales, and fins that help them move through the water.

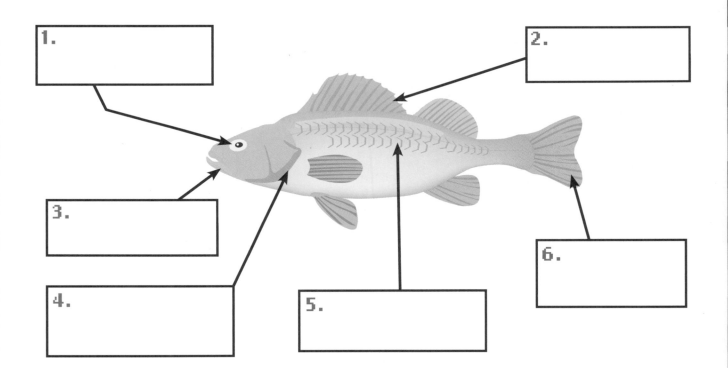

1.

2.

3.

4.

5.

6.

MINECRAFT FUN FACT

To catch a fish in Minecraft, cast a rod into water and wait. If you reel in at the right moment, you'll catch a fish.

ANIMALS/AMPHIBIANS

Read about amphibians. Then label the stages in the life cycle of a frog.

Amphibians can live in the water and on land. Frogs, toads, newts, and salamanders are some types of amphibians. Adult female frogs lay eggs. Baby frogs are called tadpoles. They are born in water and breathe through gills like a fish. When they grow legs, they are able to go on land.

adult frog	tadpole	young frog
tadpole with legs	eggs	

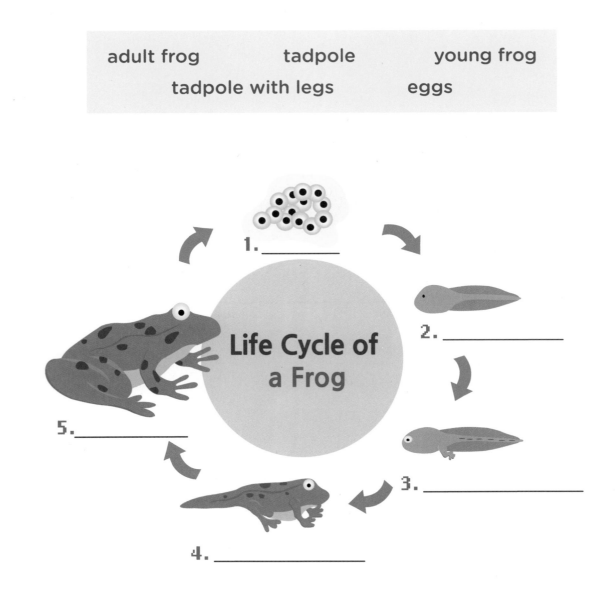

Life Cycle of a Frog

1. _____

2. _____

3. _____

4. _____

5. _____

ANIMALS/BIRDS

Read about birds. Draw a line from the first syllable to the second syllable to find bird names. Write the bird names on the lines.

Birds are a group of animals. Most birds can fly. They have wings that help them fly. They also have light and hollow bones and streamlined bodies to help them fly. Instead of teeth, birds have beaks. Their beaks are used to tear, bite, chisel, suck, crush, or chew their food.

1. par   en   _____

2. rob   trich   _____

3. tur   ven   _____

4. chick   rot   _____

5. ea   eon   _____

6. vul   key   _____

7. pen   guin   _____

8. pig   in   _____

9. os   ture   _____

10. ra   gle   _____

ANIMALS/REPTILES

Read about reptiles. Then unscramble the letters to spell some common reptile names.

Reptiles are a group of animals with some of the same characteristics. Reptiles have scales. Their scales protect their bodies. Reptiles are cold-blooded. This means their bodies change temperature depending on their surroundings. Reptiles lay eggs. Most reptiles are on their own as soon as they hatch.

1. ansek   _____

2. retlut   _____

3. gotarilla   _____

4. lemonache   _____

5. dizral   _____

6. circoledo   _____

CLASSIFYING ANIMALS

I wonder how scientists classify me.

Draw a line between the type of animal and its characteristics.

1. mammal

2. bird

3. reptile

4. amphibian

5. fish

A. is covered with scales, lays eggs, is cold-blooded

B. is covered with scales, lives in the water and breathes using gills, lays eggs

C. is covered with hair, gives birth to babies, breathes with lungs, feeds babies milk

D. is covered with scales, lives in water and on land, lays eggs

E. is covered with feathers, has wings and a streamlined body that helps it fly, lays eggs

MOBS AND THEIR HABITATS

Draw a line from each mob to its Minecraft habitat.

fish

cow

ocelot

chicken

donkey

snow golem

squid

polar bear

guardian

silverfish

parrot

horse

BIOMES

Read the map. Answer the questions.

Biomes of the World

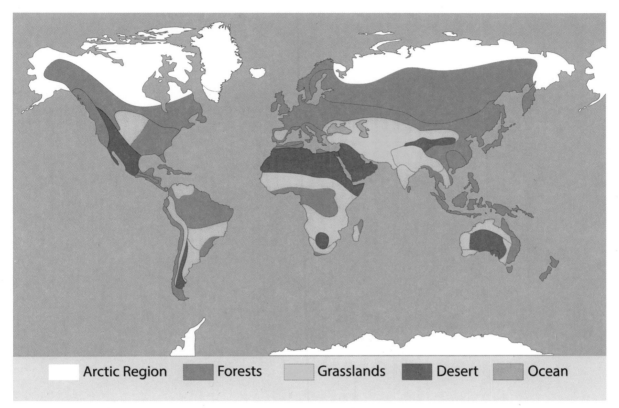

Arctic Region   Forests   Grasslands   Desert   Ocean

1. How many different types of biomes are shown on this map?

_____

2. Which type of biome covers the most area on Earth?

_____

3. Which type of biome covers the least area on Earth?

_____

4. Find where you live on the map. What type of biome do you live in?

_____

FOREST BIOME

Read about the Forest Biome. Then circle the items that are made from wood.

Just like a Forest Biome in Minecraft, forests in the real world have lots of trees. Many different types of plants and animals live in forests. There are many different types of forests. Most tropical forests are located near the equator. Tropical forests get lots of rain. The boreal forests, or taiga, are the largest forests. They have regular seasons but stay cool most of the year. Many forests are becoming smaller because of logging. Wood from trees is used to build many things.

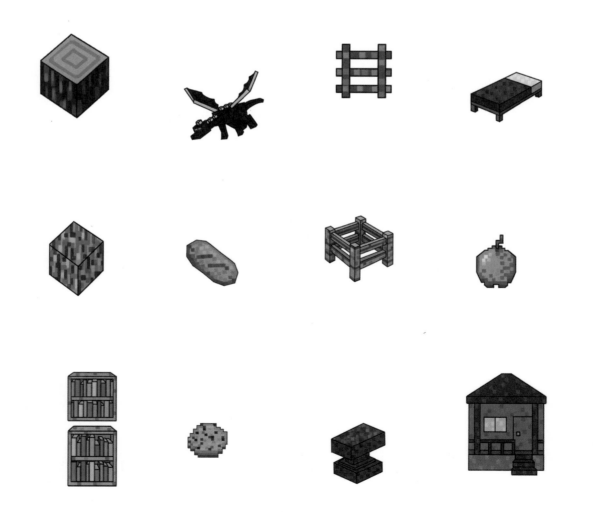

GRASSLANDS

Read about the grassland biome. Look at one food chain from the grasslands. Fill in the blanks.

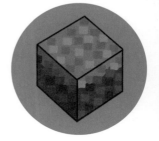

Most of the grassland biomes are located near the equator. The grasslands are named for the tall grasses that grow on the flat land. Many plants and animals live in grasslands. There are grasslands on every continent.

1. The sun provides food for the

_____ .

2. The grass provides food for the

_____ .

3. The grasshopper provides food for the

_____ .

4. The bird provides food for the

_____ .

5. The snake provides food for the

_____ .

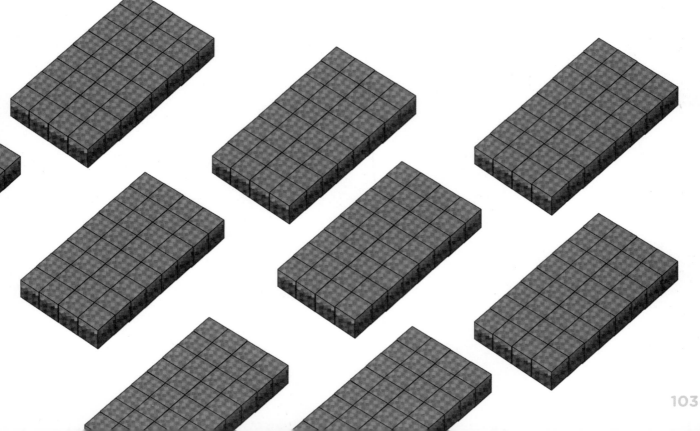

ARCTIC BIOME

Read about the Arctic Biome.
Circle seven animals hidden in the Arctic.

The Arctic Biome is very cold. Temperatures are below freezing all year. In the real world these biomes are located near the North and South Poles. Plants and animals have special ways of adapting to the cold.

DESERT BIOME

Read about the desert. Draw a line to match how each plant or animal adapts to a hot desert.

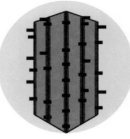

The desert biome is very dry. It gets very little rainfall. Temperatures in some deserts get very hot. Plants and animals have found special ways to adapt to the desert.

1.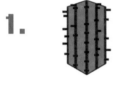

A. It slithers quickly across the sand.

2.

B. It stores water inside its trunk.

3.

C. It uses very little water.

4.

D. It burrows in sand by a rock.

OCEAN BIOME

Read about the ocean. Then unscramble the letters to spell the names of some ocean animals.

Most of the Earth is covered by ocean biome. The ocean is cold and salty. There are five ocean biomes—the Pacific, Atlantic, Indian, Arctic, and Southern. Many types of plants and animals live in the ocean.

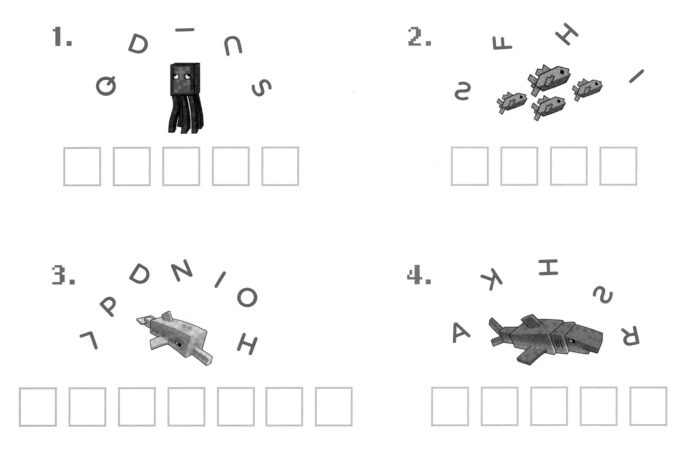

1.

2.

3.

4.

LAKES & RIVERS

Read about lakes and rivers. Then look at the chart showing the longest rivers in the world and answer the questions.

Lakes are bodies of water surrounded by land. Lakes form when rivers or streams find their way into a basin. Most lakes contain fresh water from rivers. Rivers and streams carry water and sediment to lakes. The sediment takes up space and gradually fills the lake. Reservoirs are lakes that are made by humans. They store water for later use.

Lengths of the Longest Rivers

Amazon	4,345 miles
Nile	4,258 miles
Yangtze	3,915 miles
Yellow	3,395 miles
Mississippi	2,320 miles

1. How long is the longest river in the world?

_____

2. How much longer is the Amazon River than the Nile River?

_____

3. How long is the Mississippi River?

_____

4. Which is longer: the Yellow River or the Yangtze River?

_____

MOUNTAINS

Read about the types of mountains. Then unscramble the letters to label each mountain.

A mountain is a landform that rises high above the land. There are five types of mountains: dome, volcanic, plateau, fold, and fault-block. Each type of mountain is formed in a different way.

1. DOFL

_____

2. TFULA-OKCBL

_____

3. CANCVOLI

_____

4. MDOE

_____

5. ALPATEU

_____

THE SUN, AIR, AND WATER

Read about the sun, air, and water. Follow the directions to label and color Earth.

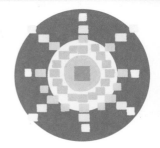

Earth is a pretty cool planet. Like other planets in our solar system, Earth orbits around the sun. Life exists on Earth because of the sun, the air, and water. Without the right amount of heat from the sun, the right air to breathe, and water, there would be no life on Earth. And without life on Earth, there would be no Minecraft world!

1. Color the oceans blue.

2. Color the land green.

3. Add the sun to show its position from Earth.

WEATHER

Read about weather. Use the weather words to answer the riddles.

Air and water are all around us. The sun provides heat. It warms the air and water. Weather describes the air, water, and heat that surround us. When we talk about the weather, we use words like sunny, rainy, windy, snowy, hot, and cold. Weather changes daily. Weather is different in different places. Weather is different in different seasons. Weather affects how we dress and what we do. Weather affects how we live.

| wind | cloud | rain | hail | snowflake | thunder | lightning | temperature |

1. I clap without any hands. What am I? _____

2. I can be a gentle breeze or a strong gust. What am I? _____

3. I am little balls of frozen snow. What am I? _____

4. I may be flaky, but I am one of a kind. What am I? _____

5. I drop from way up high. When the sun shines I make a bow across the

   sky. What am I? _____

6. I light up the sky on a dark stormy day. What am I? _____

7. I rise up and down but never move. What am I? _____

8. I may look fluffy like a pillow but I am all wet. What am I? _____

CLOUDS

Read about clouds in the real world. Tell the area and perimeter of the Minecraft clouds. Each side of a square = 1 cm.

When the sun heats the water, the water rises and forms clouds. Clouds are made of small water droplets. Clouds form when the temperature in the sky cools. There are three main types of clouds—cirrus, stratus, and cumulus. Cirrus clouds are high and thin. Stratus clouds look like flat sheets. They cover most of the sky. They usually bring rain. Cumulus clouds look soft and puffy. White cumulus clouds mean good weather. Gray cumulus clouds mean rain.

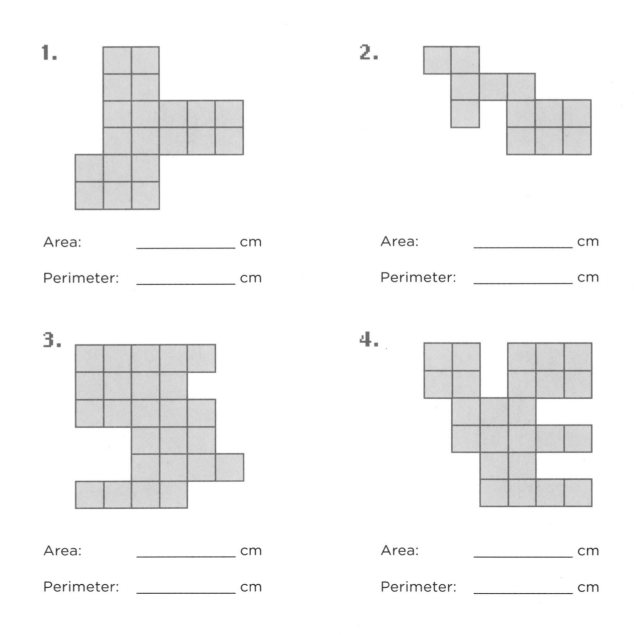

1.

Area: _____ cm

Perimeter: _____ cm

2.

Area: _____ cm

Perimeter: _____ cm

3.

Area: _____ cm

Perimeter: _____ cm

4.

Area: _____ cm

Perimeter: _____ cm

PRECIPITATION

Read about precipitation. Complete the acrostic puzzle with words about precipitation.

Clouds form from water that evaporates from the earth. When the temperature of a **cloud** cools, it creates precipitation. **Precipitation** is water that falls from the clouds. Waterdrops are called **rain**. When clouds get even colder, the waterdrops turn to **ice** or **snow**. Sometimes rain will freeze as it falls. This is called **sleet**. Sometimes when snow falls, it collects more water on the way down. The wind carries the snow back up to the clouds, where it freezes again. This forms ice balls or **hail**.

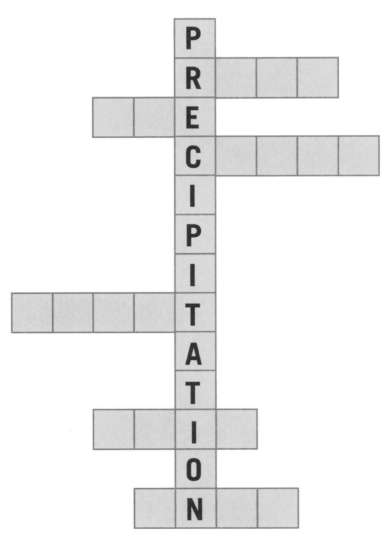

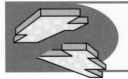

MINECRAFT FUN FACT
Weather in Minecraft changes only for a few seconds. Then it goes back to normal.

WEATHER FORECASTING

Look at the forecast for weather in the Minecraft world. Use the key to answer the questions.

Minecraft Weather Forecast

jungle

mountains

farm

swamp

Weather Key

sunny

cloudy

windy

rainy

1. Where would be the best place for a picnic today?_____

2. Where will you need your umbrella today? _____

3. Where will the sun **not** be shining?_____

4. Where will you need to hold on to your hat? _____

ENERGY

Read about energy. Draw a line to match each picture to its energy source.

Energy is how things move and change. Plants need energy to grow. People need energy to move. Machines need energy to work. There are many types of energy. Some energy is found in nature. Some energy is made by humans. The sun is one energy source. It provides plants the energy to grow. People need food to make energy. Lights need electricity to shine. Cars need gasoline or other fuel to run. Heat and wind are other sources of energy.

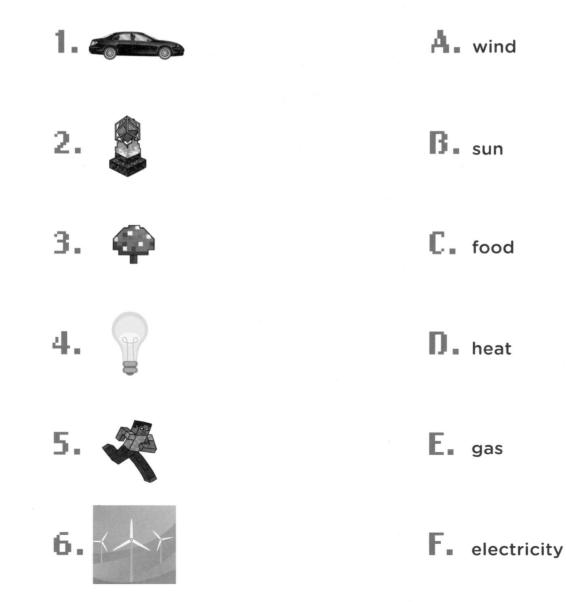

1.   **A.** wind

2.   **B.** sun

3.   **C.** food

4.   **D.** heat

5.   **E.** gas

6.   **F.** electricity

HEAT ENERGY

Read about heat energy. Tell about the heat energy in each picture.

Heat energy is all around us. The sun produces heat energy. The sun keeps us warm. Heat energy causes water to move through the water cycle. We also use heat energy to cook. Fire is a source of heat energy. Fire creates heat to warm us. Fire uses heat to make things melt.

1. How does the torch use heat energy?

_____

2. How does rabbit stew use heat energy?

_____

3. How does the thistle use heat energy?

_____

4. How does nitwit use heat energy?

_____

5. What will happen to snow golem if it heats up?

_____

6. What will happen if zombie falls in lava?

LIGHT ENERGY

Read about light energy. Then answer the questions by circling yes or no.

Light is a source of energy. The sun, fire, and electricity all produce light. Light energy travels in waves. It helps us see. It produces colors. Light cannot pass through opaque objects. It can only pass through transparent objects. When light is blocked, it makes a shadow.

1.  The door is opaque. Can light pass through the door?　　Yes　　No

2.  Does the sun produce light?　　Yes　　No

3.  The window is transparent. Can light pass through the window?　　Yes　　No

4.  Do torches produce light?　　Yes　　No

5.  Witch can see his shadow. Is witch transparent?　　Yes　　No

SOUND ENERGY

Read about sound energy. Draw some sound waves.

I like to make loud SSSSSSounds!

Sound is a type of energy caused by vibration. Sounds moves through the air in waves. Loud sounds have more energy and vibrate faster than quiet sounds. Pitch is how high or low a sound is.

This wave shows a high pitch.

This wave shows a low pitch.

This wave shows a loud sound.

This wave shows a quiet sound.

1. Draw a sound wave that shows Alex whispering to pig.

2. Draw a sound wave that shows ghast screeching.

FORCE AND MOTION

Read about force and motion. Answer the questions.
Write to explain your answer.

Objects stay at rest until a force causes them to move.
Objects can be pushed or pulled. It is easier to pull a heavy object
because there is less friction. The heavier an object is, the more
force it takes to move it. More force makes objects move faster.

1. Which object would take more force to move?

_____

2. Would it be easier to push or pull a cow?

_____

3. Which object would you rather have fall on your head?

_____

4. Will going uphill or downhill make the minecart go faster?

_____

FORCE AND MOTION

Read more about force and motion. Answer the questions.
Write to explain your answer.

It takes force to slow or stop a moving object. It also takes force to change the direction that an object is moving in. Friction is a force that slows objects down. Gravity is a force that pulls objects to the ground.

1. Describe a force that Alex might use to stop a spider crawling on her wall. _____

2. Describe a force that brings a ball tossed in the air back to the ground.

   _____

3. Skeleton throws bones on the track. Describe how the bones will act as a force against Steve's cart.

   _____

   _____

4. Alex and Steve are riding downhill in their minecarts toward each other. Explain what will happen.

   _____

   _____

I was the first mob in the Minecraft!

THE FIRST AMERICANS

Read about Native Americans. Then find the names of some of the Native American tribes in the puzzle.

Long before the United States was a country, Native Americans lived on the land. They lived in communities or tribes. They worked, built homes, and found food. They had families. They had their own language and culture. Culture is the way a group of people live. The culture of a tribe depended on the natural resources from the land.

Cherokee	Chinook	Iroquois	Shoshone
Hopi	Sioux	Navajo	Pawnee
Apache	Comanche	Pueblo	Mohawk
Cheyenne	Blackfoot	Shawnee	

```
K O O N I H C E E N W A P Z
D E Z Y I X N N B N P Y V Y
R Y H P Z O W L K W A H O M
Z I O C H V A T E J Q R T Z
A H R S N C H E R O K E E Q
Z P O O K A N S P D N T D M
W H A F Q W M U I N L O T W
S L O C A U E O E O J Q L N
D O L H H B O Y C A U K T X
T B S M L E E I V L W X W P
Z M G O M H T A S Y T T M T
R Q D J C J N T M Y J J J N
```

120

NATIVE AMERICAN HOMES

Read about some of the different types of Native American homes. Draw a line to match each home to its description.

Minecraft houses are built with blocks.

Native Americans built their homes from the materials available where they lived. Tribes in forest areas used trees to build their homes. Tribes in the desert areas used clay to build their homes. Tribes in the plains used animal skins to build their homes. Some tribes moved from place to place to find food. Their homes were easy to move.

1. Longhouses are made of logs and trees. Many families can live together in one longhouse.

A.

2. Teepees are made of animal skins wrapped around long poles. They are easy to move from place to place.

B.

3. Pueblos are made of clay. The clay makes the homes cool.

C.

4. Wigwams are made of trees and animal skins. They are round. They stay in one place.

D.

NATIVE AMERICAN FOODS

Minecraft food is crafted.

Read about some of the different types of Native American foods. Then unscramble the words to complete each sentence.

Native Americans ate foods from the natural resources around them. Tribes in forest areas ate nuts, berries, and animals. Tribes in the desert planted corn, beans, and squash. These crops could grow in the hot, dry land. Tribes on the plains ate lots of meat. Tribes that lived near rivers and oceans ate a lot of fish.

1. Pueblo tribes lived in the desert. They planted _____,
oncr

_____, and _____.
nseab   **qashsu**

2. Blackfoot tribes lived on the plains. They ate meat from

_____.
uflafbo

3. Chinook tribes lived near rivers and the ocean. They ate

_____.
shif

4. Chinook tribes lived near rivers and the ocean. They ate

_____, _____, and small _____.
tuns   **rebreis**   **linamas**

122

NATIVE AMERICAN CRAFTS

Look at some of the different types of Native American crafts. Draw about one of your favorite crafts below.

I craft many weapons and tools.

totem poles

pottery

dreamcatchers

masks

blankets

My favorite craft is _____ .

A group of bats is a colony.

THIRTEEN COLONIES

Read about the thirteen colonies. Circle the names of the thirteen colonies in the puzzle.

Before there was the United States, there were thirteen colonies. Virginia was the first colony. It was founded in 1607. People from all over Europe settled in the colonies. Each colony had its own history and way of life. England had control over the thirteen colonies.

Connecticut	Pennsylvania	Massachusetts	Georgia
Maryland	Virginia	New Hampshire	New Jersey
New York	Delaware	Rhode Island	North Carolina
			South Carolina

```
M A S S A C H U S E T T S A N
R A V P E N N S Y L V A N I A
T M N L R Y E Z G Z N I D N R
X U L I M H T W V E L B E Y B
Y Q C T L G O I J O O W Y X B
D K T I B O R D R E H R W K T
M R W X T G R A E A R R G X Y
D A T D I C C A M I Q S Z I J
E M R N N H E P C T S N E D A
L B I Y T E S N L H V L M Y T
A A P R L H W M N Y T J A Z N
W L O T I A L Y W O V U Y N M
A N Y R P Y N T O R C X O L D
R R E G Z T T D L R W G B S T
E Q N T B K N R Q J K K R L L
```

MAP OF UNITED STATES

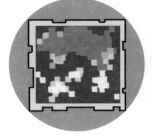

Read the map. Answer the questions.

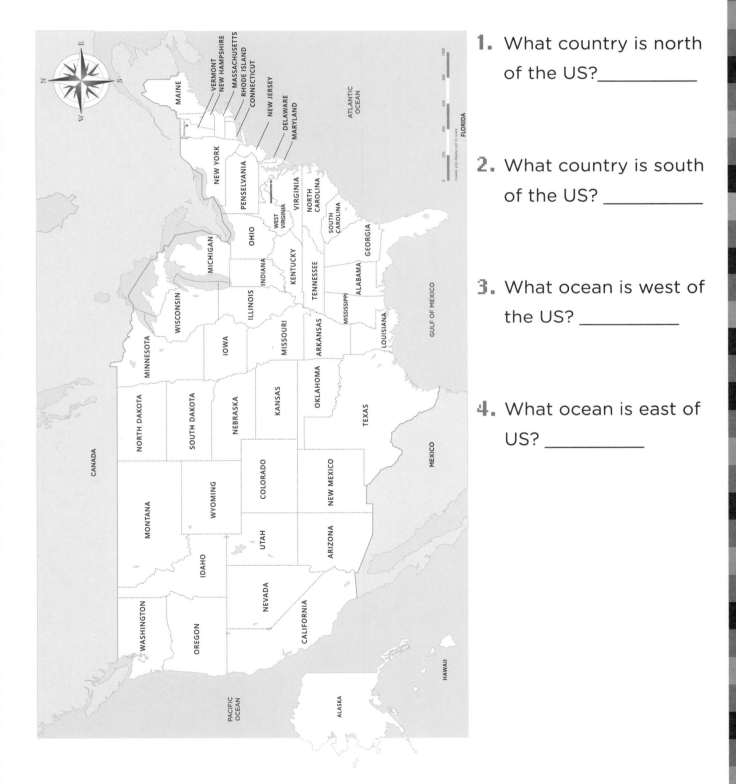

1. What country is north of the US?_____

2. What country is south of the US? _____

3. What ocean is west of the US? _____

4. What ocean is east of US? _____

REGIONS OF THE UNITED STATES

Learn about the regions of the United States.

The United States is a large country. It has 50 states. It is divided into five regions or parts. The regions are based on geography, climate, and history.

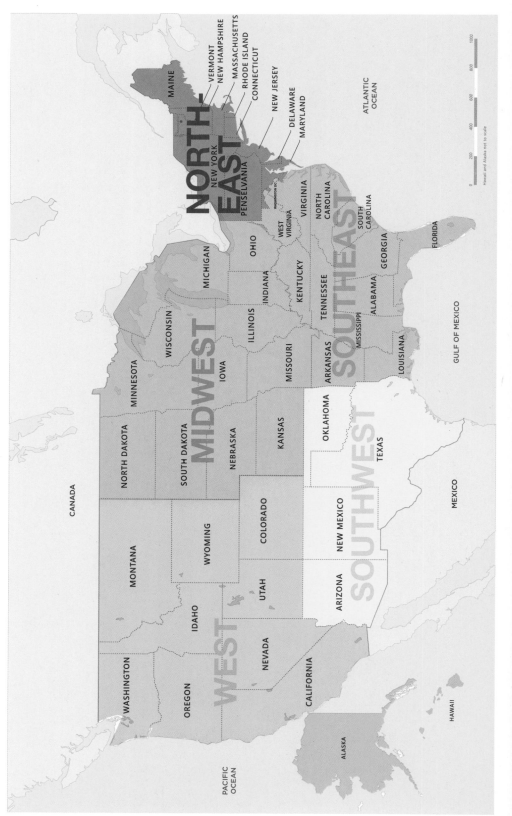

REGIONS OF THE UNITED STATES

Write the names of the states in each region. Put a star on your state on the map on page 126.

1. WEST

_____ _____ _____

_____ _____ _____

_____ _____ _____

_____

2. MIDWEST

_____ _____ _____

_____ _____ _____

_____ _____ _____

_____

3. SOUTHWEST

_____ _____ _____

_____

4. SOUTHEAST

_____ _____ _____

_____ _____ _____

_____ _____ _____

5. NORTHEAST

_____ _____ _____

_____ _____ _____

_____ _____

CONTINENTS OF THE WORLD

Look at the map. Read the clues to label the continents.

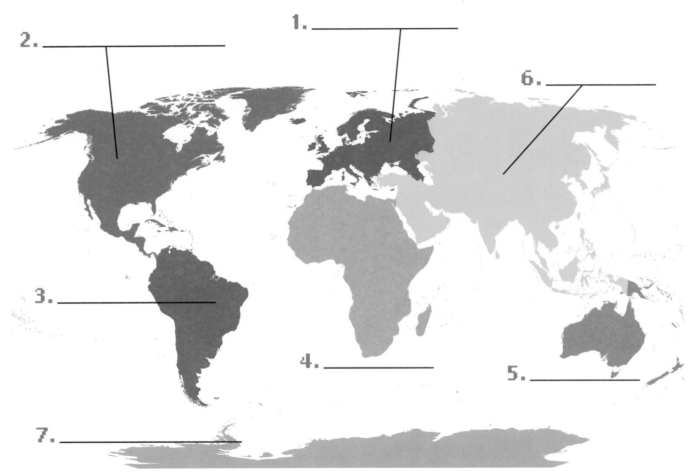

1. _____

2. _____

6. _____

3. _____

4. _____

5. _____

7. _____

Australia is the smallest continent.

North America is made up of the United States, Greenland, Canada, and Mexico.

South America is below North America.

Asia is the largest continent.

Europe and Asia share the same land mass. They are separated by mountains.

Africa is below Europe and Asia.

Antarctica is the southernmost continent.

WONDERS OF THE WORLD

Read about the Seven Natural Wonders of the World. Match each image to its description.

1.  2.  3.  4.

5. 6. 7.

_____ Parícutin is a volcano in Mexico.

_____ Victoria Falls in Africa is the largest waterfall.

_____ Mount Everest in the Himalayas is the highest mountain.

_____ The Great Barrier Reef in Australia is the largest coral reef.

_____ The Grand Canyon is located in the United States.

_____ The northern lights are a natural light show that can be seen in the Northern Hemisphere.

_____ The Harbor of Rio de Janeiro in Brazil is the largest bay.

COUNTRIES

Read about countries. Use the map on the opposite page to answer the questions.

A country is a nation with its own government. There are more than 190 countries in the world. Some countries are small, and other countries are large.

1. What country is also a continent?_____

2. What is the largest country in the world? _____

3. Name two countries in North America.

_____   _____

4. Name three countries in South America.

_____   _____   _____

5. Name four countries in Europe.

_____ _____ _____ _____

6. Name four countries in Africa.

_____ _____ _____ _____

7. Name four countries in Asia.

_____ _____ _____ _____

8. Name a country you would like to visit. _____

131

COUNTRIES

Read about countries. Then, choose a country to research. Look for information in books or on the Internet to tell about the country.

A country is an area of land that has boundaries. Each country has its own government and leaders. Countries have their own culture. People in a country speak the same language. They have their own style of dress and foods they enjoy. They have their own celebrations.

_____

Name of the Country

Language : _____

Flag

Clothing

Foods

Celebrations

_____

_____

_____

_____

_____

_____

_____

_____

A COUNTRY IN THE MINECRAFT WORLD

Imagine a country in the Minecraft world. Name the country and tell about its special features. Write about the country.

_____

Name of the Country

Language : _____

Flag

Clothing

Foods

_____

_____

_____

_____

Celebrations

_____

_____

_____

_____

MAP READING

Read the map of the Arctic Biome. Then follow the directions.

Map Key

snow

cloud

frozen lake

polar bear cave

tree

rabbit hole

1. Draw an X on the polar bear cave.

2. Draw three snowballs falling from each cloud.

3. Draw a rabbit beside each rabbit hole.

4. Draw a circle around the frozen lake.

5. Count and write the number of trees. _____

MINECRAFT MAPS

Read about maps in Minecraft. Draw a picture of one of the maps. Create a key.

I am a cartographer. I make maps.

Maps help to explore new places. There are three types of explorer maps in Minecraft: woodland, ocean, and buried treasure. The maps will show a section of land where each of these places can be found. If a player is smaller than the map, it means that a player is far away from the place. These maps can be found in Creative mode.

Title of Map : _____

Map Key

PEOPLE TO KNOW: BENJAMIN FRANKLIN

Read about Benjamin Franklin. Then circle the words in the puzzle that tell about his life.

Benjamin Franklin was a writer and a scientist. He helped write the Declaration of Independence and the US Constitution. He also wrote about the weather. By watching lightning during a storm, he learned about electricity. Today his picture is on the $100 bill.

Benjamin	hundred	independence
Franklin	Constitution	lightning
writer	scientist	electricity

```
E N I M A J N E B L L N
L C R V D K R B G I O G
E N N W B R Q Q G I T D
C I L E G B Y H T K S K
T L W K D L T U T C M D
R K J R L N T T I K E P
I N M G I I E E X R W Z
C A Y N T T N P D D D W
I R G S J T E N E N Z L
T F N G I L U R P D P J
Y O Z S Y H Z M Y L N W
C X T D G R R M N Q N I
```

PEOPLE TO KNOW: THOMAS JEFFERSON

Read about Thomas Jefferson. Then unscramble the words to complete the sentences.

Thomas Jefferson was the third president of the United States. He helped write the Declaration of Independence. When Jefferson was president, the United States was small. Jefferson wanted the United States to grow. He bought a large piece of land from France. It was called the Louisiana Purchase. This land became about 14 states.

1. Jefferson was the third _____ .

esrnpiedt

2. Jefferson helped write the _____ .

enarotidlca fo dennepenecid

3. Jefferson bought a large piece of land from _____ .

nacerf

4. The land was called the _____ .

asoilinua cupshare

PEOPLE TO KNOW: HARRIET TUBMAN

Read about Harriet Tubman. Then answer the question.

Harriet Tubman was born a slave. She ran away from her slave owners. She helped many slaves run away from their slave owners. She planned a way for escaped slaves to travel to the North safely. They did this by staying with friendly families along the way. The route they took was known as the Underground Railroad.

What did Harriet Tubman do to help slaves?

_____

_____

_____

_____

_____

_____

_____

PEOPLE TO KNOW: SITTING BULL

Read about Sitting Bull. Complete the acrostic with words that tell about Sitting Bull.

Sitting Bull was a Native American **chief**. He was the **leader** of a **Sioux tribe**. He was brave. **Gold** was found on his tribe's land. The Americans wanted the gold. Sitting Bull would not leave the land. His tribe went to war against the Americans. But still Sitting Bull would not leave the land. He lived up to his name.

PEOPLE TO KNOW: GEORGE WASHINGTON CARVER

Read about George Washington Carver. Circle T for each sentence that is true. Circle F for each sentence that is false.

George Washington Carver was born a slave. Because he was often sick, he couldn't work in the fields. Instead he studied plants. When slavery ended, George went to school. He did many science projects with plants. He studied peanut plants. He made many things from peanuts. He became known as the Peanut Man.

1.	Carver was born a free man.	T	F
2.	He loved to play in the fields.	T	F
3.	He studied plants.	T	F
4.	His favorite plant to study was corn.	T	F
5.	Carver was not able to go to school.	T	F
6.	His nickname was the Peanut Man.	T	F

PEOPLE TO KNOW: AMELIA EARHART

I'd like an airplane to fly through the Minecraft world.

Read about Amelia Earhart, and review the timeline.
Then answer the questions.

Amelia Earhart loved to fly airplanes. She set many flying records. She wanted to become the first woman to fly around the world. During her 1937 flight, her plane disappeared. She was never found.

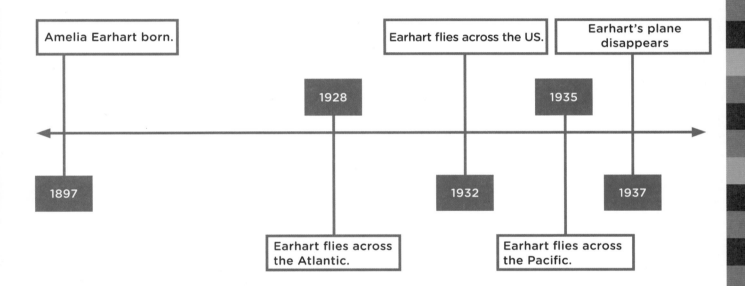

Amelia Earhart born.

1928

1897

Earhart flies across the Atlantic.

Earhart flies across the US.

1935

1932

Earhart flies across the Pacific.

Earhart's plane disappears

1937

1. What year did Earhart fly across the Atlantic Ocean? _____

2. What did Earhart do in 1932? _____

_____

3. What year did Earhart fly across the Pacific? _____

4. What happened to Earhart in 1937? _____

_____

OUR GOVERNMENT

Read the chart to learn about the groups or branches of our government. Complete the sentences.

Our Three Branches of Government

LEGISLATIVE BRANCH	EXECUTIVE BRANCH	JUDICIAL BRANCH
makes laws	carries out laws	evaluates laws
Includes senators and representatives from each state	The President is the head of the executive branch	Includes Supreme Court and other courts

1. The three branches of our government are the _____, ____

_____, and _____.

2. The President is the head of the _____ branch.

3. The _____ branch is made up of the courts.

4. The _____ branch makes the laws.

CHECKS AND BALANCES

Read about our government's checks and balances.
Complete the chart.

Our government has three branches. Each branch checks on the power of the other branches. This is called checks and balances. The system of checks and balances makes sure that no branch becomes too powerful. The President in the executive branch can veto laws and declare a kind of law called an Executive Order. The **executive branch** can decide on the judges and grant pardons. The **legislative branch** can impeach the President, must agree to the President's cabinet members, and determines how money is spent. They must agree to the appointed judges and can impeach judges. They can also overturn a presidential veto with enough votes. The **judicial branch** decides if the executive and legislative branches are making Executive Orders and laws that are fair according to the Constitution.

Executive Branch	Checks on the Legislative Branch	Checks on the Judicial Branch
Legislative Branch	Checks on the Executive Branch	Checks on the Judicial Branch
Judicial Branch	Checks on the Executive Branch	Checks on the Legislative Branch

US CONSTITUTION

Read about the US Constitution. Complete the graphic to show how rules and laws are alike.

Laws for a country are like rules in a family. Laws and rules help people live together and get along. The US Constitution is the law of our country. It was written by a group of leaders more than 200 years ago. It tells how our country will run. It tells how our country can be a fair and safe place for everyone to live.

Rules in Your Family	Laws in Our Country

How Rules are Like Laws

BILL OF RIGHTS

Read about the Bill of Rights. Put a star by the right that you think is most important and write to explain its importance.

A right is the freedom to live as you want, as long as you obey laws. Some writers of the U.S. Constitution did not think the laws in the Constitution protected the rights of people. So they added the Bill of Rights to the Constitution. The Bill of Rights include many rights for people. Some of the rights include:

Freedom to say what you want to say.

Freedom to choose your religion or no religion.

Freedom to protest.

Freedom to vote.

Freedom to fair procedures and trials if arrested for a crime.

_____

_____

_____

_____

ECONOMIC RESOURCES

Read about economic resources. Circle to tell if the picture is a human, natural, or capital resource.

People need resources to live. There are three types of resources: human resources, natural resources, and capital resources. Human resources are people. **Human resources** include people who make or grow something, such as factory workers, software developers, or farmers. Human resources also include people who provide a service, such as doctors and teachers. **Natural resources** are found in nature. For example, water, trees, and rocks are natural resources that people need to live. **Capital resources** are goods that people make to be used to make and do other things. For example, computers and buildings are capital resources.

1.   human   natural   capital

2.   human   natural   capital

3.   human   natural   capital

4.   human   natural   capital

5.   human   natural   capital

6.   human   natural   capital

GOODS AND SERVICES

Complete the crossword puzzle.

I provide good eggs!

ACROSS

1 a person who makes clothes

5 a person who teaches

7 goods that include milk and cheese

8 a good used to light a room

9 a person who makes food

11 things that are made

13 a person who provides medical help

14 a good sold at a bakery

15 a person who fights fires

DOWN

1 a good used by a farmer

2 how bread is sold

3 a good that provides music in a car

4 a good used for transportation

6 a good used for word processing

10 a good you can read

11 a person who works at a grocery store

12 a job that helps people

I am going to consume this cake!

PRODUCERS AND CONSUMERS

Read about producers and consumers. Complete the chart with the missing producer or consumer.

People who make or sell goods or provide services are **producers**. People who buy or use goods or services are **consumers**. People are both producers and consumers. People are producers to earn money for the goods they need and want. People are consumers when they buy the goods and services they need and want.

Producers	Consumers
1. a bicycle shop owner	
2.	a person buying ice cream
3. a baker	
4.	a person wanting to borrow a book
5. a nurse	
6.	a person wanting to buy a house
7. a restaurant owner	
8.	a person needing new clothes

PRODUCING GOODS

Read about producing goods. Then number the steps to show how a bicycle is produced.

The production of some goods requires many different people to do their jobs. If you want to buy a bicycle, you may go to a bicycle store. But the bicycle store owner probably did not make the bicycle. Even if he or she did make the bicycle, the parts that were needed for the bicycle were probably made by someone else. There are many different types of workers who help to produce the bicycle that you buy at a store.

_____ A store owner determines how much the bicycle should cost.

_____ A truck driver transports the bicycle from the factory to the store.

_____ Buyers in a factory buy the parts needed for a bicycle.

_____ Workers in a factory build the bicycle.

_____ Bicycle designers design a new bicycle.

_____ A salesperson sells the bicycle to the consumer.

_____ Shippers in the factory get the bicycle ready to ship to the store.

_____ Advertisers advertise the bicycle.

ANSWER KEY

PAGE 5
1. long; 2. long; 3. short; 4. short; 5. short; 6. long;
7. long; 8. short; 9. short

PAGE 6
1. D; 2. A; 3. E; 4. C; 5. B

PAGE 7
1. chest; 2. shears; 3. shield; 4. thread; 5. wheat;
6. house; 7. torch; 8. bed

PAGE 8
1. B; 2. A; 3. E; 4. C; 5. D

PAGE 9

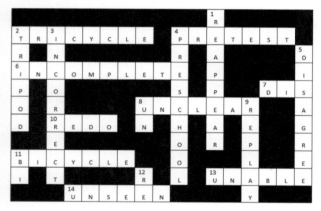

PAGE 10
1. play<u>ful</u>; 2. weak<u>en</u>; 3. care<u>less</u>; 4. avoid<u>able</u>

PAGE 11
1. sharp<u>est</u>; 2. fast<u>er</u>; 3. dark<u>er</u>; 4. cold<u>est</u>;
5. kind<u>est</u>; 6. long<u>er</u>

PAGE 12
1. 2; 2. 2; 3. 1; 4. 1; 5. 1; 6. 2; 7. 2; 8. 2; 9. 3

PAGE 13
1. glow/stone; 2. laugh/ing; 3. spi/der; 4. ap/ple;
5.la/va; 6. craft/ed; 7. beet/root; 8. puff/er

PAGE 14
1. a sunken ship; 2. magical; 3. cutting tool;
4. continuing to live

PAGE 15

PAGE 16
1. Horses eat carrots. Steve eats cake.
2. Alex rides a pig. Baby zombies ride chickens.
3. Creepers dance to the music. Creeper explodes
on the player.

PAGE 17
1. are; 2. become; 3. wears; 4. do; 5. trade; 6. like

PAGE 18
1. school; 2. family 3. bouquet; 4. swarm; 5. flock;
6. flight; 7. pack; 8. bale; 9. herd

PAGE 19
1. E; 2. D; 3. F; 4. C; 5. B; 6. A

PAGE 20
1. gave; 2. rode; 3. swam; 4. ate; 5. grew

PAGE 21

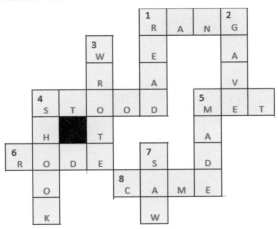

PAGE 22

Adjective choices may vary. Possibilities:
1. red <u>barn</u>; 2. noisy <u>cow</u>; 3. spotted <u>cat</u>;
4. hungry <u>horse</u>; 5. beautiful <u>butterfly</u>;
6. furry <u>cat</u>; 7. white <u>rabbit</u>

PAGE 23

1. <u>oinked</u> loudly; 2. <u>walked</u> aimlessly;
3. <u>pet</u> gently; 4. <u>hopped</u> quickly; 5. <u>sat</u> sleepily;
6. <u>floated</u> slowly; 7. <u>waited</u> patiently

PAGE 24

1. bat: a flying mammal / a stick used to hit a ball;
2. pen: an animal enclosure / a tool to write;
3. ring: the sound of a bell / a circular band; 4. fly:
an insect / to travel in the sky; 5. bark: the outer
layer of a tree / the sound a dog makes; 6. block:
a solid cube / to keep from passing; 7. sink: to go
below the water / a basin for water; 8. duck: an
animal that quacks / to move out of the way

PAGE 25

1. A; 2. B; 3. B; 4. B; 5. A; 6. A

PAGE 26

1. E; 2. G; 3. F; 4. A; 5. D; 6. H; 7. C; 8. B

PAGE 27

1. closed; 2. happy; 3. fast; 4. harm; 5. cold

PAGE 28

1. Alex, Minecraft; 2. Steve, Mindcraft Mining;
3. In, April; 4. On, Monday, Creeper; 5. Ender,
Dragon, End

PAGE 29

The Desert Biome is made up of sandstone./It is
very dry and hot. Very few plants and animals
live in the desert. Golden rabbits can live there.
Cacti can live there, too./In some deserts, there
may be a desert temple. It is usually buried
in the ground. Desert temples are dark. In the
center of the temple, there is a desert chest. It
is filled with valuable loot. At night, husks will
spawn in the desert. Many players avoid the
desert, but not Steve. He likes to visit the desert
in June when it is really hot. Sometimes Alex will
go with him. They have fun. Sometimes they look
for the desert chest.

PAGE 30

1. Steve's sword; 2. Alex's pig; 3. chickens' eggs;
4. evokers' potions; 5. villager's gems;
6. butterfly's wings

PAGE 31

1. Steve asked, "Why wouldn't the skeleton go in
the haunted house?" 2. "I don't know," answered
Alex. 3. "Because it had no guts," said Steve. Alex
and Steve laughed. 4. "That's a funny riddle,"
laughed Alex. "You are funny, Steve." 5. "I have
a lot more riddles," bragged Steve. 6. Alex rolled
her eyes. "I bet you do," she said.

PAGE 32

Answers will vary.

PAGE 33

Answers will vary.

PAGE 34

Answers will vary.

PAGE 35
Answers will vary.

PAGE 36
Answers will vary.

PAGE 37
Answers will vary.

PAGE 38
Answers will vary.

PAGE 39
Answers will vary.

PAGE 40
1. Get the creeper to come into the trap. 2. Let the creeper settle down. 3. Put a red flower on one corner of the trap. 4. Put a yellow flower on the opposite corner of the trap. 5. Open the trap. 6. The creeper will follow you. 7. You now have a tamed creeper.

PAGE 41
1. First, you'll need a shovel, some snow, a crafting table, and a pumpkin head. 2. Punch the snow with your shovel to make eight snowballs. 3. Put two snowballs in each of the two bottom left squares of the crafting table. 4. Then put two snowballs in each of the two middle left squares of the crafting table. 5. Now you have two snow blocks. 6. Put a pumpkin on top for the head.

PAGE 42

	In the corn field	Behind the haystack	In the barn	In the pen
cow	X	X	O	X
chicken	O	X	X	X
pig	X	X	X	O
horse	X	O	X	X

PAGE 43

	Hot Biome	Underwater	Nether	Forest	Village
Wolf Jockey	X	X	O	X	X
Husk	X	O	X	X	X
Zombie Pigman	X	X	X	X	O
Zombie Villager	X	X	X	O	X
Drowned	O	X	X	X	X

PAGE 44
1. D; 2. E; 3. A; 4. C; 5. B

PAGE 45
1. grow into a melon block. 2. When you find a chicken, 3. make a diamond sword. 4. When killed 5. to be friendly. 6. If you tame a pig,

PAGE 46
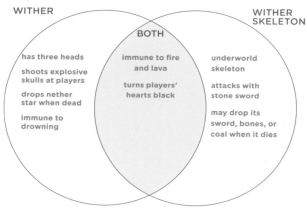

WITHER

WITHER SKELETON

BOTH

has three heads

shoots explosive skulls at players

drops nether star when dead

immune to drowning

immune to fire and lava

turns players' hearts black

underworld skeleton

attacks with stone sword

may drop its sword, bones, or coal when it dies

PAGE 47
1. 5,633; 2. 2,061; 3. 7,280; 4. 3,491; 5. 9,120; 6. 8,576; 7. 1,999; 8. 4,003

PAGE 48
1. 4,894; 2. 5,001; 3. 4,000; 4. 6,822; 5. 1,740; 6. 7,014; 7. 9,002 8. 8,221

PAGE 49
1. 400; 2. 6,000; 3. 3; 4. 800; 5. 1,000/50; 6. 900/90; 7. 3,000/1; 8. 2,000/800/30/4

PAGE 50
1. 85; 2. 72; 3. 79; 4. 67; 5. 98; 6. 66

PAGE 51
1. 88; 2. 87; 3. 99; 4. 65; 5. 97; 6. 63; 7. 93; 8. 98; 9. 86; 10. 89; 11. 79; 12. 77

FOR THE BROOM SERVICE

PAGE 52
1. 41; 2. 36; 3. 15; 4. 41; 5. 14; 6. 23

PAGE 53
1. 54; 2. 34; 3. 32; 4. 26; 5. 53; 6. 12; 7. 30; 8. 31; 9. 64; 10. 33; 11. 45; 12. 71

BLOCK THEIR PATH

PAGE 54
1. 52; 2. 72; 3. 41; 4. 95; 5. 70; 6. 82

PAGE 55
1. 60; 2. 86; 3. 83; 4. 101; 5. 95; 6. 85; 7. 105; 8. 110; 9. 71; 10. 81; 11. 84; 12. 72

BECAUSE IT HAS TEN-TICKLES

PAGE 56
1. 38; 2. 26; 3. 29; 4. 35; 5. 48; 6. 28

PAGE 57
1. 54; 2. 38; 3. 14; 4. 35; 5. 48; 6. 15; 7. 37; 8. 46; 9. 26

TO THE BAA BAA SHOP

PAGE 58
1. 52 plants; 2. 45 baby llamas; 3. 15 baby llamas; 4. 7 more diamonds

PAGE 59
1. 19 gems; 2. 102 gems; 3. 19 more diamonds; 4. 28 emeralds

PAGE 60
1. 64 spider legs; 2. 27 zombie villagers; 3. 42 skeletons; 4. 32 creepers

PAGE 61
1. 3 x 7 = 21; 2. 4 x 6 = 24; 3. 4 x 5 = 20; 4. 8 x 6 = 48; 5. 6 x 6 = 36; 6. 9 x 3 = 27

PAGE 62

x	0	1	2	3	4	5	6	7	8	9	10
0	0	0	0	0	0	0	0	0	0	0	0
1	0	1	2	3	4	5	6	7	8	9	10
2	0	2	4	6	8	10	12	14	16	18	20
3	0	3	6	9	12	15	18	21	24	27	30
4	0	4	8	12	16	20	24	28	32	36	40
5	0	5	10	15	20	25	30	35	40	45	50
6	0	6	12	18	24	30	36	42	48	54	60
7	0	7	14	21	28	35	42	49	56	63	70
8	0	8	16	24	32	40	48	56	64	72	80
9	0	9	18	27	36	45	54	63	72	81	90
10	0	10	20	30	40	50	60	70	80	90	100

PAGE 63

PAGE 64
1. 10; 2. 20; 3. 30; 4. 40; 5. 50; 6. 60; 7. 70; 8. 80; 9. 90; 10. 100; 11. 110; 12. 120

Add 0 in the ones place.

PAGE 65
1. 100; 2. 240; 3. 210; 4. 360; 5. 140; 6. 320; 7. 200; 8. 270; 9. 300; 10. 280; 11. 80; 12. 300; 13. 160; 14. 150; 15. 350; 16. 120

PAGE 66
1. 48; 2. 92; 3. 189; 4. 204; 5. 180; 6. 162; 7. 216; 8. 384; 9. 125; 10. 217; 11. 574; 12. 222

PAGE 67

1. 324; 2. 130; 3. 294; 4. 365; 5. 488; 6. 228; 7. 72;
8. 90; 9. 224; 10. 310; 11. 651; 12. 220; 13. 111; 14. 301

HE RUNS AROUND THE BLOCK.

PAGE 68

1. 4 eggs; 2. 4 withers; 3. 6 melons; 4. 7 potions

PAGE 69

1. 8 diamonds; 2. 9 emeralds; 3. 9 tin ingots;
4. 6 gold ingots

PAGE 70

1. 21/3/7/21; 2. 54/6/9/54; 3. 56/7/8/56;
4. 48/6/8/48;

PAGE 71

1. 12/4/3; 2. 42/7/6; 3. 40/5/8; 4. 36/4/9;
5. 35/5/7; 6. 45/9/5; 7. 24/6/4; 8. 63/7/9

PAGE 72

1. 40/4; 2. 80/8; 3. 30/9; 4. 60/6; 5. 60/6; 6. 70/7;
7. 90/9; 8. 70/7; 9. 80/8

PAGE 73

1. 6; 2. 9; 3. 6; 4. 4; 5. 6; 6. 9; 7. 3; 8. 7; 9. 8; 10. 7;
11. 9; 12. 3

PAGE 74

1. 8 R2; 2. 7; 3. 8 R3; 4. 6 R2; 5. 9 R1; 6. 9 R4;
7. 7 R5; 8. 6 R1; 9. 8 R4; 10. 3 R4; 11. 3 R3; 12. 6 R7

PAGE 75

1. 8 R3; 2. 5 R3; 3. 9 R6; 4. 7 R4; 5. 7; 6. 4 R5;
7. 6 R3; 8. 9 R5; 9. 6 R4

AT THE SPAWN SHOP

PAGE 76

1. 7 diamond blocks; 2. 16 diamonds and 8 sticks;
3. 8 diamond axes; 4. 31 diamonds and 24 sticks

PAGE 77

1. 8x4=32 boots/ 8x8=64 chest plates/ 5x8=40
helmets/ 7x8=56 leggings; 2. 40÷4=10 boots
or 40÷8=5 chest plates or 40÷5=8 helmets or
40÷7=5 leggings

PAGE 78

1. $3.50; 2. $7.37; 3. $12; 4. $15.63

PAGE 79

Answers will vary.

PAGE 80

1. gold block; 2. gold ingot; 3. 45; 4. 162

PAGE 81

1. gold pickaxe; 2. 11 gold ingots and 12 sticks;
3. 3 gold hoes/ 1 gold pickaxe and 2 gold shovels

PAGE 82

1. circle; 2. square; 3. rhombus; 4. triangle;
5. pentagon; 6. rectangle; 7. octagon; 8. hexagon

PAGE 83

1. F; 2. D; 3. A; 4. C; 5. E; 6. B

PAGE 84

1. 12 cm; 2. 16 cm; 3. 16 cm; 4. 18 cm; 5. 18 cm;
6. 20 cm; 7. 20 cm; 8. 16 cm; 9. 16 cm

PAGE 85

1. 18 cm; 2. 18 cm; 3. 25 cm; 4. 20 cm; 5. 64 cm;
6. 28 cm; 7. 10 cm; 8. 24 cm

PAGE 86

1. $\frac{1}{4}$ 2. $\frac{1}{2}$ 3. $\frac{4}{6}$ 4. $\frac{2}{3}$ 5. $\frac{5}{8}$ 6. $\frac{1}{3}$

7. $\frac{2}{5}$ 8. $\frac{4}{7}$ 9. $\frac{2}{4}$ 10. $\frac{4}{8}$

PAGE 87

Answers will vary.

PAGE 88

Shading of shapes will vary. 1. $\frac{6}{8}$ 2. $\frac{4}{6}$; 3. $\frac{4}{8}$;
4. $\frac{3}{12}$; 5. $\frac{2}{3}$; 6. $\frac{2}{8}$; 7. Two-eighths and one-fourth
are equivalent fractions; they equal the same
amount of pie. Eighths are smaller slices than
fourths, so in this case, it's not true that 2 is more
than 1.

PAGE 89

1. artery; 2. lungs; 3. liver; 4. large intestines;
5. brain; 6. vein; 7. heart; 8. stomach; 9. small
intestines

PAGE 90

1. pupil; 2. cornea; 3. lens; 4. retina; 5. optic nerve

PAGE 91

1. outer ear; 2. sound waves;
3. it begins to vibrate; 4. the nerves

PAGE 92

1. E; 2. B; 3. H; 4. F; 5. D; 6. G; 7. I; 8. C; 9. A

PAGE 93

Answers will vary.

PAGE 94

```
R D O N K E Y N W
N W D O F X E O R
R G R L C K C P J
P A O Z C E A D H
E W B I M M L O P
E P H B A R R O X
H C T L I S P B T
S R L A E T I J P
B B P L C D G J T
```

PAGE 95

1. eye; 2. fin; 3. mouth; 4. gill; 5. scales; 6. tail

PAGE 96

1. eggs; 2. tadpole; 3. tadpole with legs;
4. young frog; 5. adult frog

PAGE 97

1. parrot; 2. robin; 3. turkey; 4. chicken; 5. eagle;
6. vulture; 7. penguin; 8. pigeon; 9. ostrich;
10. raven

PAGE 98

1. snake; 2. turtle; 3. alligator; 4. chameleon;
5. lizard; 6. crocodile

PAGE 99

1. C; 2. E; 3. A; 4. D; 5. B

PAGE 100

Jungle: ocelot, parrot; Farm: cow, chicken,
donkey, horse; Underwater: fish, squid, guardian,
silverfish; Arctic: snow golem, polar bear

PAGE 101

1. 5; 2. ocean; 3. desert 4. Answers will vary.

PAGE 102

PAGE 103

1. grass; 2. grasshopper; 3. bird; 4. snake; 5. owl

PAGE 104

PAGE 105

1. B; 2. D; 3. A; 4. C

PAGE 106

1. squid; 2. fish; 3. dolphin; 4. shark

PAGE 107

1. 4,345 miles; 2. 87 miles; 3. 2,320 miles;
4. Yangtze River

PAGE 108

1. fold; 2. fault-block; 3. volcanic; 4. dome;
5. plateau

PAGE 109

PAGE 110

1. thunder; 2. wind; 3. hail; 4. snow; 5. rain;
6. lightning; 7. temperature; 8. cloud

PAGE 111

1. A: 20, P: 24; 2. A: 12, P: 22; 3. A: 25, P: 30;

4. A: 24, P: 36

PAGE 112

PAGE 113

1. on the farm; 2. in the jungle; 3. in the jungle and
in the mountains; 4. at the swamp

PAGE 114

1. E; 2. D; 3. B; 4. F; 5. C; 6. A

PAGE 115

1. to create light; 2. to cook; 3. to grow; 4. to stay
warm; 5. It will melt. 6. It will die.

PAGE 116

1. no; 2. yes; 3. yes; 4. yes; 5. no

PAGE 117

Pictures will vary. 1. Waves will be low and wide.
2. Waves will be high and close together.

PAGE 118

1. anvil; 2. pull; 3. feather; 4. downhill

PAGE 119

Answers will vary. Possible answers: 1. Putting
an object in front of the spider 2. Gravity causes
the ball to come back down. 3. The bones cause
friction. 4. They will crash.

PAGE 120

```
K O O N I H C E E N W A P Z
D E Z Y I X N N B N P Y V Y
R Y H P Z O W L K W A H O M
Z I O C H V A T E J Q R T Z
A H R S N C H E R O K E E Q
Z P O O K A N S P D N T D M
W H A F Q W M U I N L O T W
S L O C A U E O E O J Q L N
D O L H H B O Y C A U K T X
T B S M L E E I V L W X W P
Z M G O M H T A S Y T T M T
R Q D J C J N T M Y J J J N
```

PAGE 121

1. D; 2. B; 3. A; 4. C

PAGE 122

1. corn/beans/squash; 2. buffalo; 3. fish; 4. nuts/berries/animals

PAGE 123

Answers will vary.

PAGE 124

```
M A S S A C H U S E T T S A N
R A V P E N N S Y L V A N I A
T M N L R Y E Z G Z N I D N R
X U L I M H T W V E L B E Y B
Y Q C T L G O I J O O W Y X B
D K T I B O R D R E H R W K T
M R W X T G R A E A R R G X Y
D A T D I C C A M I Q S Z I J
E M R N N H E P C T S N E D A
L B I Y T E S N L H V L M Y T
A A P R L H W M N Y T J A Z N
W L O T I A L Y W O V U Y N M
A N Y R P Y N T O R C X O L D
R R E G Z T T D L R W G B S T
E Q N T B K N R Q J K K R L L
```

PAGE 125

1. Canada; 2. Mexico; 3. Pacific Ocean;
4. Atlantic Ocean

PAGE 126–127

1. Hawaii, Alaska, California, Nevada, Utah, Colorado, Oregon, Idaho, Wyoming, Montana, Washington; 2. North Dakota, South Dakota, Minnesota, Wisconsin, Nebraska, Iowa, Illinois, Indiana, Michigan, Ohio, Kansas, Missouri; 3. Arizona, New Mexico, Texas, Oklahoma; 4. West Virginia, Virginia, Kentucky, Arkansas, Tennessee, North Carolina, South Carolina, Georgia, Alabama, Mississippi, Florida, Louisiana; 5. Pennsylvania, Maryland, Delaware, New Jersey, Connecticut, Rhode Island, New York, Massachusetts, Vermont, New Hampshire, Maine

PAGE 128

1. Europe; 2. North America; 3. South America; 4. Africa; 5. Australia; 6. Asia; 7. Antarctica

PAGE 129

1. The Grand Canyon is located in the United States. 2. Mount Everest in the Himalayas is the highest mountain. 3. Parícutin is a volcano in Mexico. 4. The Harbor of Rio de Janeiro in Brazil is the largest bay. 5. Victoria Falls in Africa is the largest waterfall. 6. The northern lights are a natural light show that can be seen in the Northern Hemisphere. 7. The Great Barrier Reef in Australia is the largest coral reef.

PAGE 130–131

Many answers will vary; 1. Australia; 2. Russia

PAGE 132

Answers will vary.

PAGE 133

Answers will vary.

PAGE 134

5. 10

PAGE 135

Answers will vary.

PAGE 136

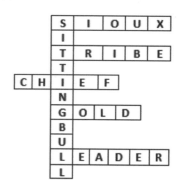

PAGE 137

1. president; 2. Declaration of Independence;
3. France; 4. Louisiana Purchase

PAGE 138

Exact answers may vary but include:

She planned a way for escaped slaves to travel to the North safely.

She created the Underground Railroad.

PAGE 139

PAGE 140

1. F; 2. F; 3. T; 4. F; 5. F; 6. T

PAGE 141

1. 1928; 2. She flew across the US; 3. 1935;
4. Her plane disappeared.

PAGE 142

1. legislative/executive/judicial; 2. executive;
3. judicial; 4. legislative

PAGE 143

Answers may vary.

PAGE 144

Answers may vary.

PAGE 145

Answers may vary.

PAGE 146

1. capital; 2. human; 3. capital; 4. natural;
5. natural; 6. capital

PAGE 147

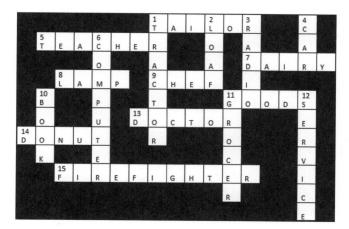

PAGE 148

Sample answers are provided. 1. a kid wanting a new bike; 2. an ice cream shop owner; 3. a person who wants a birthday cake; 4. a librarian; 5. a person who is sick; 6. a realtor; 7. a hungry family; 8. a clothing store owner or a tailor

PAGE 149

1. Bicycle designers design a new bicycle.
2. Buyers in a factory buy the parts needed for a bicycle. 3. Workers in a factory build the bicycle. 4. Shippers in the factory get the bicycle ready to ship to the store. 5. A truck driver transports the bicycle from the factory to the store. 6. A store owner determines how much the bicycle should cost. 7. Advertisers advertise the bicycle. 8. A salesperson sells the bicycle to the consumer.